How To Occupy Till Jesus Comes

Wealth Creation

- Y. E. SHOFOLA -

An environmentally friendly book printed and bound in England by www.printondemand-worldwide.com

Mixed Sources
Product group from well-managed forests, and other controlled sources
www.fsc.org Cert no. TT-COC-002641
© 1996 Forest Stewardship Council
FSC

PEFC Certified
This product is from sustainably managed forests and controlled sources
www.pefc.org
PEFC
PEFC/16-33-415

This book is made entirely of chain-of-custody materials

FastPrint Publishing
www.fast-print.net/store.php

How To Occupy Till Jesus Comes – Wealth Creation

A catalogue record for this book is available from the British Library

ISBN 978-178035-549-8

First published 2013 by
FASTPRINT PUBLISHING
Peterborough, England.

This book is dedicated to God the Father, God the Son (Jesus Christ), and God the Holy Spirit.

The Lord has done this and it is marvellous in our eyes.

PSALM 118:23 (KJV)

Acknowledgements

To my number one fan in the world, the best mother in the whole universe. I love you Mum and thank you for your continual spiritual support, guidance, and unconditional love. I decree longevity and sound health into your life and you will make Heaven in the name of Jesus (Amen).

To my spiritual mentor and father in the Lord, Dr D.K. Olukoya: a true General of the Lord's Army for the end time revival. Your spiritual lifestyle never ceases to motivate and challenge me to be a better Christian. I decree longevity and perfect health into your existence in the name of Jesus. You will go from ultimate anointing to explosive anointing in the name of Jesus. The God of Elijah will uphold you to the very end and you will make Heaven in Jesus' name (Amen).

To Vince Stanzione, thank you for the support given to write this book. I decree long life and divine health into your body, soul and spirit in Jesus' name (Amen).

Disclaimer

The Author and the Publisher have taken the utmost care and effort to check the information and advice in this book; nevertheless, with a book as comprehensive as this one and the fact that things do change, the Author and the Publisher cannot be responsible for any loss that you may suffer as a result of any omission or inaccuracy.

Contents

Introduction

We were created to have dominion on this earth, that is, to occupy in all that we do. Even in the face of the recent global economic downturn we still need to occupy our rightful positions on earth.

"And God said, let us make man in our image, after our likeness: and let them have dominion over the fish of the sea, and over the fowl of the air, and over the cattle, and over all the earth, and over every creeping thing that creepeth upon the earth. So God created man in his own image, in the image of God created He him; male and female created He them. And God blessed them, and God said unto them, be fruitful, and multiply, and replenish the earth, and subdue it: and have dominion over the fish of the sea, and over the fowl of the air, and over every living thing that moveth upon the earth." Genesis 1:26-28 (KJV)

Through non-compliance with God's instruction our fore parents in the Garden of Eden renounced the dominion of this earth that was handed to them by the Most High God to Satan. Praise God! Dominion was restored back to mankind through the Lord Jesus Christ. 'For if by one man's offence death reigned by one; much more they which receive abundance of grace and of the gift of righteousness shall reign in life by one, Jesus Christ. Therefore as by the offence of one judgment came upon all men to condemnation; even so by the righteousness of one the free gift came upon all men unto justification of life.' Romans 5:17-18 (KJV). Jesus came that we might have life and to have it in abundance.

In this global financial meltdown many people have been flooded with debts and lost their livelihoods. At the same time, a small group of people with certain skill sets have been stockpiling their wealth, even in these times of uncertainty. The few lucky ones with jobs are tired of going to their regular job every day, just knowing that they're doing nothing more than just working to get by. We know how the 9 to 5 job feels and we all know it's like the modern day slavery.

We all know deep down in our hearts that we can't depend on any jobs these days because you never know when it's time for redundancies or job cuts - it can happen all of a sudden. If you were to get laid off tomorrow, do you have a plan B to plan Z to support yourself and your family? 'What's the way out?' I hear you ask.

King Solomon, in his proverbial words of wisdom, shares with us his experiences as the wisest and richest man the world had ever known; his observations about the purpose of life are in the book of Ecclesiastes 11:1-6 (GNT).

He encourages us to "Invest your money in foreign trade, and one of these days you will make a profit. Put your investments in several places - many places even - because you never know what kind of bad luck you are going to have in this world. No matter which direction a tree falls, it will lie where it fell. When the clouds are full, it rains. If you wait until the wind and the weather are just right, you will never plant anything and never harvest anything. God made everything, and you can no more understand what he does than you understand how new life begins in the womb of a pregnant woman. Do your planting in the morning and in the evening, too. You never know whether it will all grow well or whether one planting will do better than the other."

From the Bible passage above, one can imagine that the merchants in the days of Solomon took huge risks. They invested in a cargo of wheat and sent it out across the waters to a foreign port in the hope of trading the grain for precious stones, spices and almug wood. If the ship returned with such a cargo it could be sold off, making a huge profit for the merchants.

It was not easy for a merchant to risk all on an overseas trading mission. The ship sailed out of his control. He relied upon the expertise of others - particularly the captain of the ship. The cargo was at the mercy of the weather; there was an awful lot of ship wrecked. Merchants would often make a total loss. Pirates frequented the seas. Cargoes were stolen. Ship captains were often dishonest. There certainly weren't any insurance policies to cover losses. And to top it off, there was a long wait to see if you were going to make any money, usually from six to ten months, but on occasion, upwards of three years. Why would merchants take these risks? The merchants took the risk because the reward was great and believed that "nothing ventured, nothing gained." This advice is timeless and is practical for all people and all ages in our generation.

Using this illustration, King Solomon is encouraging us to be risk takers. Unfortunately, only a few Christians dare to be bold with their lives and '*carpe diem*' (Latin word which means to 'seize the day') by understanding that each new day is a fresh gift from God. Life itself is a gift from God and God wants us to enjoy every single day of it.

The Parable of the Pounds

Here is the famous Parable of the Pounds. Jesus told this story to his followers in the closing days of his ministry, when many of them mistakenly expected the kingdom of God to suddenly appear. This parable lays out an investment strategy for the followers of Jesus Christ. The parable can be found in the Gospel according to St. Luke 19:11-27 (KJV)

"And as they heard these things, he added and spake a parable, because he was nigh to Jerusalem, and because they thought that the kingdom of God should immediately appear.

He said therefore, A certain nobleman went into a far country to receive for himself a kingdom, and to return. And he called his ten servants, and delivered them ten pounds, and said unto them, 'Occupy till I come.' But his citizens hated him, and sent a message after him, saying, 'We will not have this man to reign over us.' And it came to pass, that when he was returned, having received the kingdom, then he commanded these servants to be called unto him, to whom he had given the money, that he might know how much every man had gained by trading. Then came the first, saying, 'Lord, thy pound hath gained ten pounds.' And he said unto him, 'Well, thou good servant: because thou hast been faithful in a very little, have thou authority over ten cities.'

And the second came, saying, 'Lord, thy pound hath gained five pounds.' And he said likewise to him, 'Be thou also over five cities.' And another came, saying, 'Lord, behold, here is thy pound, which I have kept laid up in a napkin: For I feared thee, because thou art an austere man: thou takest up that thou layedst not down, and reapest that thou didst not sow.' And he saith unto him, 'Out of thine own mouth will I judge thee, thou wicked servant. Thou knewest that I was an austere man, taking up that I laid not down, and reaping that I did not sow: Wherefore then gavest not thou my money into the bank, that at my coming I might have required mine own with usury?' And he said unto them that stood by, 'Take from him the pound, and give it to him that hath ten pounds.' (And they said unto him, 'Lord, he hath ten pounds.') 'For I say unto you, that unto every one which hath shall be given; and from him that hath not, even that he hath shall be taken away from him.' But those mine enemies, which would not that I should reign over them, bring hither, and slay them before me."

Here is the picture of a very opulent aristocrat who is leaving on a long trip to a distant land. He expects to be gone for many years but eventually he will return. In the meantime, he calls ten of his most trusted servants together and gives them a pound each and instructs them to buy, sell and trade with the pound. It means to use the pound to make more money, invest it and not sit on it. In our day it applies to entrepreneurship, stock and commodities trading, crude oil exploration, internet marketing, property developments, importing and exporting, franchising, etc.

"Calling ten of his [own] bond servants, he gave them ten minas [each equal to about one hundred days' wages or nearly twenty dollars] and said to them, Buy and sell with these while I go *and* then return." Luke 19:13, (AMP).

The Assignment

So off went the opulent aristocratic on his long journey back to the headquarters to get authorisation for his rule and then to return. For an easy understanding, I call the servants; Mr Risk Taker, Mr Cautious and Mr Foolish, they joyfully waved their master off. Mr Risk Taker prayed unto God for His divine guidance on how to invest his entrusted money and God answered him speedily and sent him vision helpers to assist him. Mr Risk Taker took bold steps immediately and did not give any room for the spirit of procrastination. He exercised his vehement faith in the Lord and soon had a ginormous portfolio of diverse investments.

Likewise Mr Cautious prayed unto God for His divine guidance on how to utilise his entrusted money and God answered him speedily and sent him vision helpers to inspire him. Mr Cautious educated himself on the latest investment opportunities in order to make informed decisions on where to invest his delegated money. He became overwhelmed with all the wonderful opportunities around him. But he systematically weighed all the pros and cons of all the opportunities that would yield a great return on investment before he carefully invested his entrusted money.

Meanwhile Mr Foolish after he has received his charged money, leant on his own understanding, he did not pray unto God for guidance on how to utilise his entrusted money. He quickly hatched a wonderful plan in his heart on just what to do with his allocated money. He locked his bedroom door to ensure that no one was looking, he carefully wrapped his assigned money in a beautiful piece of scarf and he hid the money in his cellar. What a foolish man indeed!

Retribution day

After the departure of the opulent aristocratic back to the headquarters, slowly days turned into weeks, weeks turned into months, months turned into decades and even decades gradually turned into centuries. Alas! There was no sign of the opulent aristocratic. Mr Foolish was now very comfortable and happy with his phlegmatic decision. He was somehow convinced that the Master will never be back. Nevertheless, he would periodically sneak into the cellar to check if the money was still intact. Each time he was happy to find the money beautifully wrapped just the way he had left it. He was confident that peradventure his master should come back he would be proud of his custodian initiative. However, he was baffled and could not honestly comprehend while the other two servants were working their guts off especially now that their Master had been away for several centuries. Meanwhile Mr Risk Taker and Mr Cautious were busy investing their money in securities, financial trading, oil exploration, internet marketing, property developments, importing and exporting, franchising, etc.

Then one beautiful spring day it was business as usual; people were going about their personal businesses, the G8 countries were having their annual summit discussing global issues, Wall Street Hedge Fund Managers closing multi-million dollars deal, Farmers harvesting their crops into the barns, old aged pensioners walking their dogs in a nearby field, parents playing with their children in local parks, newly wedded couples going on honeymoons, pregnant women in antenatal clinics, and some people in funeral parlours organising burial ceremonies for their departed loved ones.

Suddenly, there was a beautiful deafening sound of trumpet sound coming from the sky which caused a great pandemonium outside. Everybody rushed outside to see what was going on, cloudy dust filled the air, for a few minutes it was unclear what was behind the clouds and then suddenly from the distance came the huge cries of 'It's the Master, He's back,' ' it's the Master He's back,' 'He's the back, He's back.'

Wow! What a magnificent sight to behold, the Master in his splendour glory has returned, his long journey back to the headquarters crowned with an outstanding success. Some people recognised him and while some were clueless as to whom the Master was but they have surely heard about him. But affirmatively, the three servants whom have been entrusted with the money recognised the Master straightaway.

'And it came to pass, that when He was returned, having received the kingdom , then He commanded these servants to be called unto Him, to whom He had given the money that He might know how much every man had gained by trading.' Luke 19:15

Even though the Master had been gone for centuries, He has not forgotten the instructions that He left behind prior to His departure. He was exhilarated to see His servants so as to reward them accordingly.

The Reward

The Master quickly sent for the servants, to find out what they've done with the money He gave to each of them before His departure. The first servant came and said 'Master I doubled your money' (100% profit). He said, Good servant! Great work! Because you have been trustworthy in this small job, I'm making governor of ten cities. (Luke19:16-17) I hear you say 'cities' Yes, real cities. The first servant probably chose; London, New York, Singapore, Lagos, Tel Aviv, Cape Town, Los Angeles, Paris, Rio de Janeiro and Sydney. The second servant came and said 'Sir, your pound has earned five more.' (50% profit) His Master answered, 'You take charge of five cities.' Luke 19: 16-19. The second servant probably chose Dubai, Monte Carlo, Mumbai, Montreal, and Tokyo. Wow! What an inconceivable accolade.

The first servant's core investment portfolio was probably property development while the second servant's core investment portfolio may have been stock and commodities trading. Regardless of where they invested their entrusted money, the fact of the matter is, they both invested their money wisely and produced a fantastic return on investment for their master.

The servants were rewarded greatly beyond their wildest dreams, just by obeying their Master's simple instruction to invest the money He has left in their care.

Beloved, Jesus is the best business partner that anyone could ever wish to transact with because He does not do business like mortal men. He does not cheat. He is fair and just. Praise God!

I remember a famous Christian hymn sung in the Christendom "Let us labour for the Master from the dawn to setting sun, let us talk of all His wondrous love and care; then when all of life is over and our work on earth is done, and the roll is called up yonder, I'll be there..." Awesome! How I love that old beautiful song. When the roll is called up yonder, may we all be there in Jesus name, Amen.

Mr Foolish's Memoir

The last servant is yet to be heard from. His story is considerably different, as is the master's response. 'The next servant said, 'Master, here's your money safe and sound. I kept it hidden in the cellar. To tell you the truth, I was a little afraid. I know you have high standards and hate sloppiness, and don't suffer fools gladly.' Luke 19:20-21 (The Message)

Here is a foolish man who was wise in his own eyes. He lived by sight and not by faith. He locked his bedroom door to ensure that no one was looking, he carefully wrapped his assigned money in a beautiful piece of scarf and he hid the money in his cellar. He checked on the money periodically to ensure that it was safe and sound. He then went about gallivanting without a care in the world. One can't help but wonder why would a man behave that way? At the very least, he should have thought about depositing the money into a fixed savings account to gain some interests. Most importantly, he should have prayed and asked for God's guidance, he should have carried out a research about investment opportunities. There were so many prospects that he could have taken advantages of, but unfortunately he could not be bothered, he took his master's instruction to 'occupy till he comes' for granted.

Mr Foolish's Comeuppance

Mr Foolish's nonchalant attitude towards his Master's strict instruction to 'occupy till he comes' has finally been exposed, and there was nowhere for him to hide. No nonsensical excuses could rescue him now. He has been caught red-handed in his folly. Who will deliver him from his Master's fury? He was fearful, negligent and slothful. He played it safe and surely he's going to face the consequences. 'He said, 'You're right that I don't suffer fools gladly—and you've acted the fool! Why didn't you at least invest the money in securities so I would have gotten a little interest on it?' Luke 19:22-23 (The Message)

The Master's words spoke volume. He was furious because of the servant's nonchalant attitude. The servant did not strive to invest his master's money. He failed miserably and woefully. He was a lazy and an unproductive servant.

Utilise it or lose it

The Master is about to prove Mr Foolish right; 'Then he said to those standing there, take the money from him and give it to the servant who doubled my stake.' "They said, 'But Master, he already has double . . .' "He said, 'That's what I mean: Risk your life and get more than you ever dreamed of. Play it safe and end up holding the bag." Luke 19:24-26 (The Message)

The bystanders were dumbfounded. How can the Master be ruthless? How can he take away money from one and give it to another man? Yes, the Master can do it because it was his money after all. He was simply taking away the money the unproductive servant failed to invest. I guesstimate that the bystanders were extremely perplexed when the money was taken from Mr Foolish (who now has none) and given to Mr Risk Taker who has already been made a governor of ten cities.

Conclusion

Beloved, it's high time that we wake up from our slumber and seize the day like the first two servants that were industrious for their master. This is where this book comes in, its main goal is to bring to remembrance the Master's instruction to 'Occupy Till He Comes' , to educate and to demonstrate to God's people how to do this in a Godly way.

This book is for people that are looking for proven and tested recession proof business ideas with little start-up costs. The business ideas in this book are being used by many self-made people all over the world. This book will challenge you to move out of your comfort zone and show you how to creatively create wealth for yourself and your loved ones with minimum efforts and reaping explosive results. Lastly, the book will demonstrate how you can save money on practically everything from renting cars, to booking flights, booking hotels, utility bills, food shopping, clothes shopping, etc. God will empower you and multiply the pounds that He has entrusted into your care as you continue to occupy till He comes in Jesus name (Amen).

Prayer Points:

- Power to make wealth incubate my life in the name of Jesus, Amen.
- The Lord is my banker I shall not want in the name of Jesus name, Amen.

- Lord Jesus, bring me honey out of the rock in the name of Jesus, Amen.
- Lord, make me a channel of blessing to others in the name of Jesus, Amen.
- I am the head and not the tail in the name of Jesus, Amen.
- I am on top and not beneath in Jesus name, Amen.
- People shall compete to favour me in the name of Jesus, Amen.
- People that I do not know will serve me in the name of Jesus, Amen.
- I shall never eat the bread of sorrow all the days of my life in the name of Jesus, Amen.
- I shall lend to nations and I shall never borrow in the name of Jesus, Amen.
- The Lord shall prosper all my undertakings in the name of Jesus, Amen.
- Resources of Heaven, arise and promote my life by fire in the name of Jesus, Amen.
- I am for blessings and not for curses in the name of Jesus, Amen
- Uncommon financial breakthrough manifest in my life in the name of Jesus, Amen.
- The blessing of the Lord that maketh rich and addeth no sorrow overflow into my life in the name of Jesus, Amen.
- Jehovah Jireh, catapult my life to the mountain top in the name of Jesus, Amen.

- Where is the God of Elijah? Arise in your power and accelerate my speed in the name of Jesus, Amen.
- The sons of strangers shall build up my walls in the name of Jesus, Amen.
- Kings and queens shall minister unto me in the name of Jesus, Amen.
- Violence shall no more be heard in my land, wasting nor destruction within my borders in the name of Jesus, Amen.
- I shall suck the milk of the Gentiles and the breast of royalty in the name of Jesus, Amen.
- Strangers shall stand and feed my flocks, and the sons of the alien shall be my plowmen and my vinedressers in the name of Jesus, Amen.
- I shall feast on the bounty of nations and bask in their glory in the name of Jesus, Amen.
- My children and I are the seed which the Lord hath blessed in the name of Jesus, Amen.
- I am a stunning crown of glory in the palm of God's hand and a royal diadem held high in the hand of my God in the name Jesus, Amen.
- The descendants of my oppressors will come bowing and scraping to me in the name of Jesus, Amen.
- All who looked down on me in contempt will lick my boots in the name of Jesus, Amen.

- My caged destiny, be liberated by the power in the blood of Jesus, Amen.
- My buried glory, be exhumed by the resurrection power of the Lord Jesus Christ in the name of Jesus, Amen.
- Jehovah Jire, create divine opportunities for my prosperity today in the name of Jesus, Amen.
- Where others are spending money, I refuse to spend bold-face in the name of Jesus, Amen.
- Every evil power sitting on my prosperity somersault and die in the name of Jesus, Amen.
- Strongman at the corridor of my financial breakthrough somersault and die in the name of Jesus, Amen.
- By fire by dynamite, I take back the territories that the enemies have stolen from my life in the name Jesus, Amen.
- By fire by force I am taking over, by fire by force I am moving forward into my promised land in Jesus name, Amen.
- Witchcraft cobwebs covering my opened heaven catch fire and burn to ashes in the name of Jesus, Amen.
- Heaven over my destiny open by fire in the name of Jesus, Amen.
- Surely Goodness and mercy shall follow me all the days of life in the name of Jesus, Amen.

- I shall use my wealth to promote the kingdom of God in the name of Jesus, Amen.
- I am tired of the valley, Holy Ghost lift me up in the name of Jesus, Amen.
- Windows of Heaven open wide for my prosperity in the name of Jesus, Amen.
- God arise, and promote my destiny by fire after the order of Joseph in the name of Jesus, Amen.
- Financial embarrassment of my father's house my life is not your candidate, die in the name of Jesus, Amen.
- Stronghold of poverty, hear the word of the living God be consumed by the fire of the Holy Ghost in the name of Jesus, Amen.
- Foundational poverty your end has come, die in the name of Jesus, Amen
- My prosperity shall change the story of my father's house in the name of Jesus, Amen.
- God, arise and give me a divine leading for financial breakthrough in the name of Jesus, Amen.
- I receive the anointing for supernatural breakthrough in the name of Jesus, Amen.
- Divine acceleration my life is waiting, enter in the name of Jesus, Amen.
- It does not matter whether I deserve it or not, I receive immeasurable wealth from the Lord in the name of Jesus, Amen.
- God, arise and lift my head up in the name of Jesus, Amen.

Chapter 1

Being your own boss

Beloved, God is true to all His promises; in fact they are 'Yea and Amen'. As children of Jehovah Jireh, we have to reposition ourselves so that God can truly bless us as He has promised because He has a pleasure in our prosperity.

The Lord said He will bless all the works of our hands; God blessed the house of Potiphar for the sake of Joseph, and He blessed Laban because of Jacob. I am a living testimony of this. God richly blessed the organisations that I worked with, especially my last organisation. One year, one of my colleagues informed me in one of our monthly supervisions that her husband, who is a Hedge Fund Manager, was looking to donate some money to a worthy cause and she said they would like to donate about a million pounds. She said they would like the money to be given to my department because she loved the projects that the department was involved in. Normally this kind of donation will just disappear in the 'big budget pot'. Even after I left the organisation, this family still donates £100,000 every year. God will prosper the works of your hands whether you are an employee or an employer.

I am not going to mince my words and mess about; instead I am going to tell you straight up and it is: "You'll never get rich working for someone else". These famous words came from John Paul Getty, one of the world's richest men. The only way that you will ever make real money is to own your own business.

Yes, there are some drawbacks to being self-employed and we will go into these later; however, on balance, I guarantee you will be better off working for yourself.

Can you juggle?

Well you need to learn quickly and I don't mean with balls or oranges. Making money is like juggling — you need to juggle various qualities and areas of your life all at once. You need to juggle your mental health, physical health, your personal relationships, the actual money making, and learning how to save money.

Why owning your own business is the only option today

If you do some research and go back, say, 100 years ago, or maybe even less, you will find that nearly everyone was self-employed. Go back to your grandfather or your great-grandfather and the chances are that they worked for themselves (my grandparents were farmers with hectares of land). Many people worked from home, and in England we had the cottage industry businesses; then it all changed with the big factories etc. Fewer people were in charge of their lives and they started to rely on the big companies to look after them.

Well, we all know what's happening today — most of those big companies are disappearing or becoming smaller companies; they are breaking up into smaller divisions and the employees are being laid off. The common buzz words nowadays are 'credit crunch', 'double-dip recession', 'governmental cuts' or 'redundancies'. People who have provided 20 to 30 years plus of loyal service are being laid off.

If you are still employed at all, you will know that your employer demands more and more from you; to continually exceed your monthly targets you are expected to come in early, work late, and be responsible for your actions, and yet in good times the company rarely increases your pay or benefits, but in bad times they are quick to cut your pay, the hours you work and even lay you off.

I have recently been looking at recruitment advertisements and it amazes me what employers expect. They write long descriptions of what you must have: experience, leadership, qualifications etc., and then when you look at the benefits to you they are minimal. I see jobs advertised for directors and other senior positions that pay in one year what most successful business people would earn in a month. I am trying to demonstrate the injustice and the rewards gap between working for a real company and being your own boss.

Now throw into the equation that many employers expect you to do whatever they tell you; they still have very old fashioned ideas about who goes to the top and promotion prospects are even less. If you are a woman, black, Asian, have foreign blood in you or suffer from a disability then YOU MUST set up your own business and be your own boss.

There are a few fair employers who treat everyone as true equals, but these are very rare.

Why working for yourself is the key

Let me tell you a story about a friend, who, with a bit of help from family, set up her own business doing exactly what she used to do working for someone else. Now, she was doing OK when she worked for a company; she had a good salary + commission + car + smartphone. But she knew that if she set up on her own she would earn far more.

She was earning around £25,000 per annum plus benefits, which was not too bad. However, in her first twelve months running her own business she earned over £150,000. Now that is a true example of why you should be the boss! Sure she had to stick her neck out and take some risks, but look at the benefits.

Now back to you.

- Why are you working at the company you're with?
- Are you truly happy with your job?
- Are you being treated as you should?
- Is getting to and from work a job in itself?
- What would you do if your employer went broke or made you redundant tomorrow?

I suggest that you write the answers to these questions down and answer each one, truthfully.

How did you get into the line of work you're in?

I have asked this question to hundreds of people and most people can't answer it. It seems to me that people spend very little time on choosing their careers and employers — it is almost a case of they'll take whatever comes. I think that most people spend more time choosing a car or a house than they do selecting employment. The other reason people get into a particular profession is because of pressure from parents, a teacher, or other family members; for example, your mother or sister was a teacher so you became a teacher.

I think that there are very few people on this earth who can truly say that they are happy with their work. When I was with my last employer, which was a very large organisation, I came across many unhappy workers, some of whom had worked with the company from five to twenty-five years. They would moan about their pay, conditions, the good old days, or anything else they could think of. I asked a few of them: if things were that bad, why were they still there? Simply because they were lazy and were too scared to either challenge their employer for a better wage or to look for a new job. I am sure that many of those people are still in the same job and they are probably still moaning and complaining to themselves.

Are you working in the wrong job or business?

Most people are in the wrong profession for the reasons already mentioned. The easy way to know if you are in the right job or business is to answer a few simple questions truthfully.

1. Do you jump out of bed in the morning to go to work, or do you hate going?
2. Do you clock-watch and can't wait for breaks or for the end of the day?
3. Are you enthusiastic, motivated and proud of your work or do you do it because you have to?

4. Do your superiors motivate you and set good examples or do you find that they couldn't care less?
5. If you didn't earn any money for what you did, would you still do it?

If you are totally satisfied with your profession then congratulations — the best possible avenue for you is to become a consultant, set up your own business doing the same thing or find any other angle, such as writing a book, a newsletter or course on your profession. If you are happy with your profession, by branching out on your own you can still enjoy your profession and increase your income from it.

If you are not happy with your profession, then it is time to get out. This is where people will say, "What, at my age?" Yes, change now, because every day is another day wasted; the chances are that you were never meant to be in that profession in the first place.

If you are unhappy in your job or profession you could be doing yourself serious damage. Many unhappy people overeat, undereat, smoke, make themselves ill through stress and poor working conditions, and generally cause themselves unnecessary pain and suffering.

Analyse your skills: what makes you happy and your desires

Let's go back to the drawing board and take stock of yourself.

- What skills do you have?
- What skills would you like to obtain or improve?
- What job or profession would make you jump out of bed in the morning?
- Deep down, what was the job or profession that you always wanted to do, before others put doubts into your mind?

I believe that it is never too late to acquire new skills and to move into another profession or business which truly stimulates and excites you. Obtaining new skills is going to take some time and perseverance and you may have to attend evening classes or weekend classes after a hard day's work, but if it means improving your life, then surely it's worth it! You may also have to take another job on lower pay so that you can gain experience in your new profession, which will of course cause you financial hardship in the short term; however, the long term benefits are worth it.

Don't go through life working in the wrong profession — you will be wasting your life and all the God-given talents locked up inside you; you will never be happy or excel in a profession if your heart is not 200% in it.

Prayer Points:

1) O God of heaven and earth, help me to discover my true calling on earth in Jesus' name (Amen).
2) Master of the universe, my life is available; deposit your immeasurable talents in my life in the name of Jesus (Amen).
3) O God of Abraham, Isaac and Israel, give me power to create wealth in the name of Jesus (Amen).
4) Father Lord, reposition me to my divine position in Jesus' name (Amen).

Chapter 2

Unleashing your passionate senses

"Nothing great in the world has been accomplished without passion."

- **Georg Hegel, German Philosopher.**

You cannot become wealthy or achieve any other kind of success in life if you don't have passion about what you are doing. Be it the simplest thing or the most sophisticated thing, you need passion in order to succeed. Passion triggers the enthusiasm and motivation that give you the muscle to face the hard times. Here we take a look at how important passion is and what different forms it must take in order to point our lives in the right direction, i.e. in the direction of super success.

There are many successful people out there who are living their life as they want to. They are working hard, doing what they absolutely love to do. The most successful people are those who work toward the things they are passionate about and love. There are many reasons for this. The more you love what you do the harder you are going to work at it because you will be enjoying your work.

If you feel like you are bored with your life or not doing what you should be doing with it then it is time to make a change. There may be obstacles or fears holding you back from accomplishing the goals you have set forth in your life. It is time to get past the obstacles and make your dreams happen.

Many people aren't quite sure what their true passion is. They want to work toward being successful as they see many other people but they just aren't sure what it is that they can do. Finding your passion is possible and it will take some deep searching within yourself. Your passion may be right in front of you and you don't even realise it.

Every passion has the capability of making money. It is just seeing the angle you need to take to make it happen. You shouldn't sit around and avoid your passion because you don't think you could financially survive on it because you can.

Questions to ask yourself

Are you looking for your true passion because you seek happiness in your life or that there is a gap you need to fill? There are many questions you need to ask yourself. By carefully answering these questions will help you understand more about yourself and possibly what might be holding you back from being happy and pursuing your passions. Here are many questions you should ask yourself. You might want to get out a notepad to answer these questions or just make a mental note. Writing the answers down is usually better.

- **What really inspires and engages you?**

This question may be a little difficult to answer but you may find the answer after you finish the rest of the questions. However, you need to be very clear about where you get your inspiration from. What are the types of things you find engaging and exciting?

- **If you couldn't fail, what would you do?**

Many people don't do things because they are afraid to fail or they have failed in the past. If there is something that you would do for sure if you knew there isn't a chance whatsoever of failing what would that be?

- **If you were forced to start over again, what would you do?**

Many people find themselves in situations where they have fallen into a situation where they are not doing as they wish they were. They go to work because they have to, and not enjoying a single day of it. If you started over again would you take advantage of the new beginning or would you go back to where you are? What would you do?

- **If money wasn't an issue, what would you do?**

Many people have dreams they wish to pursue but they never attempt to move forward with the dreams because they cannot afford to get started. Think of what you would love to do if you had the money to do it. This can be anything.

- **What is your biggest dream?**

If you have a big dream, what is it? There must be something you really want to do that you dream about. Think about this one thing and focus on it.

- **What is the biggest barrier stopping you from following your dream?**

Name all the things that have caused you not to follow your big dreams. These things could be people who do not support you, money, fears, and other things. There are many different types of barriers which can be overcome. You might not see opportunity or success with your dreams or you may fear that people would make fun of you.

You might not even be skilled and lack talent. These could be barriers causing you not to move forward.

- **What passion are you afraid of owning or admitting?**

Many people have dreams and passions they are afraid to talk about out of fear of being mocked by other people. You might think your passion is daft to other people. What is this one thing?

- **As a child, what did you really want to be?**

Did you have dreams of becoming someone as a child and it didn't turn out quite as expected? Do you still wonder what it would have been like if you did follow your dreams as a child? If you had the opportunity, would you follow this dream today?

- **If you were going to die in the near future (God forbid it) what would you regret not doing?**

Many people have regrets when they realize they are going to die real soon. It is often too late for many people to go back and change the things they missed out on. They would have lived their lives completely differently if they had the chance. If a doctor told you that you hadn't any time left but a few weeks, then what would your regrets be? What would you want to do before your time was up?

Now that you have answered these questions you should have a good idea of some of the things that make you happy and your dreams. You need to have a clear idea of the things you have always dreamt to do. Knowing these things is very important.

Peak Experiences and Existing Talents

Your capabilities are very important when you are thinking about taking your dreams and making something of them. You need to think about peak experiences and existing talents you have that you can use toward the benefit of making your dreams come true. This can also help you build the confidence you need to be successful.

Your peak experiences include times in your life where you excelled. You don't have to have won an award. These peak experiences include the best times of your life. What are some of the things you have done in your life that you really enjoyed you wish you could do again? Consider some of the accomplishments you have made. You might have built things in the past when you were younger.

Existing talents you have today can be used to help you achieve your goals. Are you good at organising or marketing? You might be good at something you don't even realise you are good at. These things could be making announcements about events, making phone calls, baking, gardening, and more.

You don't have to have an expert talent. You may have the knowledge about something that you enjoy very much. Maybe you have an interest that you like to read about and this is your hidden passion. Think about something you are very knowledgeable about because you choose to be, not because you are required to be at work.

Some of the highest times in your life may be the passion you wish you had back in your life. You might have used to be a runner and always wanted to win the London Marathon but now you are lazy and have written that dream off years ago. That doesn't mean you cannot get back into shape and go for your big dream.

Everyone is good at something. If you don't have a hobby like making candles, knitting, or working on cars at the weekends it doesn't mean you don't have a skill. This just means that you haven't quite figured out what your skill is yet. You need to know what it is that interests you the most. The majority of people are very good at what they do when they enjoy it.

Using Curiosity & Creativity

One thing that is very important is curiosity because it is the base of passion. You might have understandings that are blocking you from realising what your true passion really is. Here are many ways you can use curiosity to help you determine what your true passion is so you can use it to be successful.

- **Making Your Mind Active**

Curiosity helps create an active mind. When someone is curious they always ask questions and seek for the answers. This causes their mind to be active most of the time. When you are curious and working the mind you are making it stronger. Your brain is like a big muscle and by working it you are making it much stronger.

- **Open to New Ideas**

Curiosity also allows you to see how things can be seen from different angles. When you are set in one way things are limited because your mind is not willing to accept a different solution. It is much like your life. If you don't see your life becoming any more successful than it already is then you won't be. If you can open your eyes to new ideas about how things can be then you are more willing to try them.

The great thing about curiosity is that when ideas do come to your mind they will be recognised also and not ignored. When you are not curious you miss out on the important ideas because you haven't prepared your mind to be open to them.

This also means you must be open to suggestions. Many people offer input that you might not want to hear. This input could have been the one thing that was what you needed to do in your life. Be open to suggestions by allowing yourself to ask more questions and seek different answers.

- **Open to New Possibilities**

When your mind is open to new suggestions you will also see the bigger picture in almost every situation. Your world will be open to new worlds and possibilities because you will be curious. Normally you wouldn't see these things like you see today.

It takes the most curious mind to have the capability to look beyond the normality of life and see things hidden underneath the surface. These are worlds and possibilities that you can make happen. You have total control of your curious mind.

- **Excitement**

If you are bored with your life you are most likely not curious at all. Curiosity builds excitement in your life because you will want to see things. There will always be new things that attract your attention and an abundance of toys and gadgets that you enjoy too.

When you are curious you are adventurous and it is so much fun to add adventure to your life. This doesn't mean you need to go on an African safari. It means you need to look around you and see the things that are going on a little more than you normally do. Do a little research and find out why things tick. Be curious and open to new things rather than having the same boring routine every single day.

Developing Curiosity

If you consider yourself to be curious but you are in a routine of the same thing every day and basically bored with life you are not. You are boring. You can develop curiosity to help you become a more exciting person and see the life you can have. Once you become curious and you really want to know what your life will be like when you take your passions and make them happen you will be more likely to make them happen. Here are few steps on how to:

- Keeping an open mind is the best thing you can do when you are developing your curiosity. You have to be an open minded person. If you are set in your ways most of the time, this may be the most difficult task. Work on seeing things from a different point of view. Think about different versions of things and how they could end up.
- Another thing you need to do when you are developing your curiosity is to never take things for granted. Many people accept things for how they are. They never dig deeper and they lose their entire curiosity and excitement. Many things are a really big deal and although it may seem simple to you it is important. Your child may want to do something that seems so ridiculous. It is about the time spent and you should never take these things for granted because they may not be available to you later. These

also include wasting time in your life watching television when you could be working toward your passions.

- Constantly ask questions. As you are developing your curiosity, it is important to ask questions. Who cares what people think about you? You are working on you and you need to be curious. This will allow you to get beneath the surface of things. Ask about how things work and why people are friends of each other.
- Find out as much as you can about everything. Not only are you working your brain but you are learning new things and developing an understanding also. You are learning about why people do the things they do. Although you might do something one way people may choose to do it another. This is the opening of your mind you need to do.
- Never label something as boring. If you are asked to do something with someone else and you think it sounds drab you need to get up and tackle it as if it is a lot of fun. Things are only boring that you make boring yourself. Labelling an activity or chore as boring completely closes the doors to something that might be your passion. In addition, you can think of ways to take that boring activity and make it fun.

- Look at learning as something fun. There are many things about your passion you might need to learn. You might have put off your passion because it will require you to take a few courses. It is very common for people to think they are too old to learn new things and they don't follow a passion because of this. You are never too old to learn new things. The best thing you can do is to continue learning by reading as much as you can and learning new things. You should never put a passion off because of learning. What you need to do is tackle the learning as a fun experience that is going to help you achieve a goal in the long run. Being curious is learning. You are in a lifelong class and learning new things every single day. So if you have to take a class or read a book to learn something new, tackle it with a new attitude of excitement and fun. You will learn much more than you would if you thought the learning was a burden.
- Reading new things is another way to feed your curiosity and develop it. You might like to focus on just one thing but you should be open to as many different topics and things as possible when it comes to reading. This can help you build your curiosity even further. If you do find you like to focus on just one thing then you might have found your passion.

Building Creativity

Do you think you are not a creative person? You actually might think you are creative and really not be at all. If you want to live out your passions and make them a reality then you need to be creative. There are many ways you will need to creatively tackle barriers and make things happen. The more creative you are the more successful you will be in your life. Here are a few ways you can build creativity in your life:

- Make creativity a game in everything you do. When you come upon a circumstance you should give yourself the rules. Think about the objectives and any obstacles or strategic constraints that might be a problem. The more creative you are with these answers the better you are.
- When you are creative you also have to set goals. Goals go with deadlines and you need to set a deadline with activities. When you attach a deadline with tasks it actually makes them more exciting. You also won't procrastinate as much either.
- Self-expression is a very important aspect also. You need to find every opportunity to express yourself that you can in a creative fashion. Not only in a creative fashion but in every opportunity. When you look for opportunities to express yourself you are being creative in the process. Expressing yourself can be in the way you display

dinner on the plate. You might choose to dress up the meal with cranberries and garnishes. You may change the way you do a presentation at work and completely changing the style from the way your work does it. View every activity as a way to express yourself and be creative.

- Allow more focus in your life. The best things you can do for yourself is to eliminate distractions and noise when you focus on an activity. When you focus on an activity really hard you will see opportunities and qualities about it. If you really cannot pay attention to something then it really is boring. Again, find ways to make it exciting.
- When you are working on activities that seem like they are boring then you should view them as smaller pieces of a bigger picture. You need to see the big picture of things and every aspect of an activity.

Walk around your home

If you are having a hard time figuring out what your true passion is, it may be sitting right in front of you. You may have collections of items like figurines, magazines, hobbies you like to do on the weekends and more. Take a look around your home and see if some of the decorations are a clue to what your true passion is. You might be surprised you have surrounded yourself with items and not even realised it.

Barriers

Many people are very clear what their passion is but they have external barriers that are in the way. If you have barriers that are stopping you from living out your dreams then you need to get past them. You have full control of external barriers and you can do something about them.

- **People**

The biggest barrier to someone not fulfilling their passion and dreams is another person. It is common for someone to add input that is hard to listen to because you feel like you are being made fun of. A person may ridicule the idea, think it is silly, and much more. The last thing you need to listen to is an outside opinion if it is negative. If you have a passion you need to surround yourself with supportive people. Someone who is not supportive is not who you want around because they will only bring you down. That is, if you let them.

Many people have a spouse that is not supportive of a passion because they think the idea is ridiculous or they would be embarrassed of what your passion is. This type of person you don't need around you. If you are making a decision of your spouse over your passion then you are restricting yourself. It is important to make it clear to your spouse that you are passionate about doing something in particular and they need to be supportive of you.

When you have the right support you can do anything. When family members are not supportive emotionally then it can make things difficult. The best thing you can do is let them know you are fulfilling your dreams and they will not stand in your way. It is your life and you need to be satisfied with it when the time comes. You may have to shut out unsupportive people for a while until they see that it truly makes you happy.

- **Money**

Money is one of the biggest barriers that cause people not to move forward with a passion. You might be an excellent mechanic and you want to start your own shop but you have never moved forward with the idea because of the cost. Money can be overcome.

There are many ways to get money together to start your own business or live out a passion that might cost a lot of money. The best thing you can do is begin cutting costs in your life where you don't need them.

Many of the ways you can cut costs in your life include not eating out every day for lunch at work. Pack a lunch. Consider taking the bus and not driving in everyday so you don't have to costs for petrol and parking. Think about many of the additional expenses you have that you really don't need. You might buy tons of extra things at the grocery store you don't even eat but it happens because you always go grocery shopping when you are hungry.

Every time you save money you would have normally spent on something like, a lunch at work you need to put the money away. Open a savings account or buy a lock box at home and put the money in it. Don't count the money or ever get into it. Just remember that every time you are adding to the box you are getting closer to achieving your passion.

One thing to remember is that by being creative with your life you will most likely find other ways you can make additional money to put aside for your endeavour. You also may find a way to start your dream without any start-up costs. There are many home businesses ideas discussed later in this book with little or no start-up capital. If you love to make aromatherapy candles and you have always dreamed of owning your own shop then you can start a business online first. You may even find your online business is more successful than a brick and mortar store would ever be.

Money is an obstacle that can be overcome. It is the most common excuse people use for why they cannot live out their dreams. You should never fear for your survival. In addition, if you have a supportive spouse they will help with the financial burden while you are getting started so you can live out your dreams. In most cases, the financial pay-out in the end will be much better.

- **Time**

Another reason many people do not live out their passions and make them happen is because they say they do not have the time. This could be close to true if you commute to work hours away and get home late at night. It is common for many people to be slaves to their work and never have time even for their family. This makes them feel selfish when they want to take time out to live out a desired passion.

If time is a problem you must find a way to make time in your life to do what it is that you want to do. You might consider waking up an hour or two earlier every day or staying up just a little bit later. Remember, sleep is important for happiness and a good day so you cannot cut too much into your sleep.

You might get an hour for your lunch break and can bring crafts with you to work or your laptop to work. This way you can work on your passion an hour each day. Finding the time is very important.

Time wasted is very common for people who claim they do not have the time to live out their passions. You might spend hours every night watching television and not doing very much on the weekends either. This time might be your relaxing time because you work so hard during the week.

It is time to start cutting out all of the time wasted in your life going out with your friends, watching television, and doing things that are not productive. You do have time to get started. You just need to manage your time better. Remember that you don't have to complete an entire project once you get started. If your project is hours and you have an extra hour each day then you can do a little bit at a time. This will allow you to have something to look forward to each day also.

- **Job**

If your current job is the reason you cannot live out your passions because you are currently a slave to your employer then you should find a new employer. If you are not doing what you love to do in the first place then it won't matter if you find another employer.

Your job may be your livelihood but you need to work toward being happy with your life and successful. When your job is the reason you cannot be happy you won't even be successful at your job. You won't move up and you will despise it. It may be very hard to wake up every morning to go to work each day. Don't you want to do something that you enjoy waking up in the morning each day for? You can and you have full control over this.

- **Fears**

Fear is another one of the biggest reasons people do not move forward with their passions and make their dreams reality. You can overcome fears and you need to overcome them. By the power of curiosity you will be more open to suggestions and know that there can be a better outcome than what your mind has limited you to believe.

You might have a fear of failing and this is why you have not moved forward with your passions. If you fear failing it is natural. It is like learning how to ride a bicycle or learning something new. Not many people start something new or take on a passion and immediately are successful. There are many fears and failures along the way you will experience. You have to pick yourself back up and keep it going.

Being afraid to fail is normal and you don't have to let it stop you. When you fail you need to take it on as a learning experience so you can grow from it. Failure can be turned into a positive experience.

You might even have a fear of success. That might sound funny but many people are afraid to succeed. They have problems saving money but as soon as they start to save, they ended up squandering the saved money on something they don't even need. Later they are kicking themselves and begin the saving process all over again.

You should never be afraid to succeed. This fear is natural and many people have a self-esteem low enough they don't believe they are good enough to be successful. You can be as successful as you really believe you can be. Don't let your fears of what could be getting in the way.

- **Learning**

Learning is another obstacle for many people. You might have finished school 20 years ago and figure you are done with learning anything new. This is silly and you are always capable of learning even when you are 80 years old. You need to take on the entire learning process as a fun and exciting thing. You will be living out your dreams soon and if it requires you to obtain a certification or learn something then you need to look at this as a stepping stone toward your goals.

There are many obstacles that you can say are the reason for you not living out your dream. These are only temporary barriers that you are using as an excuse for not moving forward. You are in control of barriers and your mind. You have control of the people in your life who are supportive or not. You have control over your job or the ability to creatively find ways to fund your endeavours. Barriers can creatively be overcome to get started with living out your passion. You need to stand up and say no more to barriers that are in your way and start living your dreams.

Goal Setting

Goal setting is important for many reasons. When you set goals you can see forward progress, you have something to look forward to, and they help create ambition. You must set goals in order to achieve them.

When you set goals the best thing you can do is attach a date on different milestones. Take a specific goal of your passion and attach a completion date to it. Upon a completion date, you will then break down your goal into many steps to get you there. Each of these steps is a milestone. You might consider putting a date on each milestone based upon how long they will take you to get to. These might be estimated dates and you might be off by a day or two. However, one milestone may be accomplished quicker than another so it can put you back on track.

Working by using a goal method gives you something to look forward to. The best thing you can do is reward yourself at the end of each goal or you may be seeing the reward as you are getting closer to your passion actually happening. When you are working toward a completion date you are more likely to work on the goal rather than say I plan on getting it done eventually. A date makes the goal more real.

Goals with milestones allow you to see the forward progress you are making toward achieving your goal. You might consider making a chart with the dates and step attached to it. Break down each step with tasks you need to complete and things that need to be done. As you reach each milestone you will be closer to reaching your goal.

The closer you get to achieve your true passion the more ambition you will have to live out the dream and make it happen. If you need to brush up on your skills first then take a few classes. These classes will be a part of your milestones and steps to get to where you want to get to. As you complete each one then you will have completed a milestone and closer.

If your goals include steps that are very difficult to do and require a lot of hard work on your part do not be afraid to reward yourself for getting to where you are in your project. Take the night off and celebrate for reaching a goal. Do something to treat yourself for your hard work. You deserve it and you are worth it.

For any project you decide to tackle or any endeavour you want to achieve you need to design it as a goal with a breakdown of the steps to get to the goal. This will make the goal look so much easier to get to and you will work harder to achieve it. In addition, you have a way to measure just how close you are to actually making it happen in your life what you have always dreamt of.

Living Your Passion

When you live out your passions there are many things you need to do with your attitude and your life in order to be successful. You will be a more successful individual with life and your passions when you practice these things.

You can measure success any way that you want to. Success is not measured by money because anyone can make a lot of money. The goal is to make a lot of money by living out your passion. When you are working toward something you are extremely passionate about you will usually be fortunate enough to make some money. The important thing is that you can look back on your life and know you did everything you wanted to do and you have no regrets.

- **Be Whole**

Your passion needs to make you whole. You need to focus on not just one thing but every aspect of your passion. Enjoy the experience in its entirety. Enjoy the process of ordering the parts and having them delayed for two weeks. This could mean a wonderful vacation for you while you are waiting rather than a sign you weren't supposed to get started on your passion. Don't look at negative things happening as a sign. Be whole with everything you do. Don't try to be fake or impress someone with someone you are not.

- **Be Passionate**

When you are passionate about something you don't have to be a display of passion so other people can see you. Your passion comes from inside and if you truly love what you are doing then this will come naturally for you. You will take pride in your work and if you design clay pots then you won't send a cracked pot out to a customer because you will be passionate about the quality. This is because you will own it and your name will be on it. You will be proud of everything you do because you are proud of this.

- **Leadership**

Jesus is the best example of leadership. He came to earth to fulfil with one agenda i.e. to redeem the human race from eternal damnation. He never erred from His agenda. He fulfilled it. He never removed His focus from it despite the distractions and temptations. We can all learn from Jesus's style of leadership. He lived a passionate life. He wholehearted loves the children of men that He gave His for them.

- **Continuous Improvement**

As you are living your passion you will not be putting out the best every single time. You need to find ways to continuously improve processes that are slowing you down, causing poor quality, or frustrating you. When you continue to improve the process you will do better as time goes by and begin to see how well you can do. Productivity improves after time once you find ways to make things better. When you first start off with your passion everything may seem in disarray and a mess. You can fix this but it will take time and trials. You may try something fifteen times before you hone a method down to the most productive and quality method.

- **Action**

Action needs to be all around you when you are living your passion. Because it has been so easy to procrastinate to work toward your passion you do not want to fall into the same problem as before. It is important to take action with yourself, people you include to help you and more.

Taking action is the most important thing to avoid procrastination. You want to work toward a big goal which is your dream. Nothing is going to get in your way or slow you down. Put a sign up that says action to remind yourself you are working toward your passion by constant action.

You want to have people on your team that are action oriented also. Don't have people work with you that are not action oriented. If you have a really supportive aunt that likes to sit around and talk but not work hard then you cannot have her help you with your passion. She may be the person you can have help you create hype for your endeavour or business but not to take action. Find a place for her so she can help because you need the support.

Always reward action. Never let action and goal setting go without rewards. You want to reward everyone helping you and yourself. This doesn't mean you need to spend money you don't have. You can reward someone by letting them know you appreciate what they are doing for you.

Acknowledgement of hard work is sometimes enough when people know you really appreciate it.

- **Choose a mentor**

Never underestimate the power of mentoring. Choose one or two mentors who are successful in their chosen field. Study everything you can about them and become an expert on them. Learn about how they became successful. This means you should know their entire autobiography.

Turning Passions and Goals into Reality

Turning your passions into reality requires you to do many things. Now that you know how to find your passion and live your passion you need to make your passion really happen. Here are things you can do to make it happen:

- **Believe**

The just shall live by his faith (Habakkuk 2:4). The most important thing to success is to believe that you will be successful. You really can be successful but if you do not believe it then you shouldn't even get started until you do. Your abilities are in your mind and you have total control over your success. It is not about impressing people. You can believe and you don't have to tell anyone. Relax and believe you will be very successful and one day you will be so excited to write a book or hold seminars and talk about your passion and how you turned it into a reality. Believe and feel empowered as you think about your endeavour and how you are going to be successful.

- **Attitude**

Your attitude could make you or break you. You need to maintain a complete positive attitude. Be positive at all times. Don't let the little things get you down or upset you. You are living your passion and every obstacle now is a learning experience. Now you need to have a positive outlook on everything you do with your business and your passion.

When you have a good attitude it will help you become more successful with your business and your passion. You need to have a positive outlook and believe. When your attitude is positive and your outlook is positive things will begin to work in your favour more often than they ever have before. It is really about the way you look at things and not how bad they really are. Your attitude is what will make it positive.

- **Hone Your Idea**

If you are in a situation where you cannot make your passion a reality today then you will need to hone your intentions. You can take your idea and make it better by chiselling away at the details. Lay out the plan for your project or business endeavour and every detail you will need to consider. When you are in a waiting period there are still plenty of things for you to do. Don't look at a waiting period as a sign you shouldn't get started or as another way to procrastinate.

- **Build Momentum**

The best way to build momentum when you are working toward your passion is to act on the ideas you have. Act right away and don't sit around for something to happen or come to you. The same goes for a problem you need to fix. You need to act on it. The more responsive you are then you begin to build a momentum that is hard to break. Your laziness will go away and you will do well with being more productive.

- **Make the Best of Your Resources**

When you are making it happen then you need to make the best of your resources. You might not have a lot of money so you need to be resourceful, manage the little and make it last. You can find family members, friends and other supportive individuals to help you. If you are short on supplies you might have to talk to friends and people to see where you can get a hold of more supplies. You may not have money or resources you need. You need to be creative about things you can do. If you are a writer without a computer then you can go to the public library and use a free one. Find resources that you can use to make your passions successful.

- **Sacrifice and Hard Work**

In most cases when someone works toward a passion they are prepared to work hard and willing to sacrifice just about anything. When you first start off with your new job you might find that you are very poor to begin with. You cannot expect to be a success overnight. Things will take time but the importance is that you will be doing what you enjoy. You will be required to work long hours and relinquish many other things. Sacrifice is the most important thing you can do if you want to be successful.

There is no substitute for hard work if you want to reach your goals. Only you can reach the goals you set for yourself and you will need to work very hard to get to where you want to be. Embrace long hours, sweat and tears because they will be rewarding in the end. 'Those who sow with tears will reap with songs of joy. Those who go out weeping, carrying seed to sow, will return with songs of joy, carrying sheaves with them.' Psalm 126:5-6 (NIV)

- **Organise Your Life**

Organise your life around your passion. You have started a new job or passion that you want to be successful in. Start living the successful day that you have always dreamt of. For example, wake up early in the morning, have your quiet devotional time with the Lord, brew coffee, read the paper, do the school run, talk on your blog, and more. Plan your time with plenty of exercise and healthy decisions. Be sure you are getting enough sleep also. You will have to put in a lot of hours to be successful at first but you cannot lose sleep or you will have problems enjoying your passion. Working towards a passion means you get to sleep too. Proper organising will allow you to be successful and more productive.

Visualisation and Meditation

Visualisation is very important if you want to work towards your passion. Meditation in the word of God helps you see where you are going with your passion. 'Keep this book of the law always on your lips; meditate on it day and night, so that you may be careful to do everything written in it. Then you will be prosperous and successful.' Joshua 1:8 (NIV) If you have an idea, visualise it, believe it, and pray it into manifestation. 'If you can imagine it, you can achieve it. If you can dream it, you can become it.' **William Arthur Ward**

Conclusion

- A passion is something that you want to do and you were meant to do with your life. Everyone has a passion and they can live a full life when they know exactly what their passion is and what they need to do.
- Success is not measured by money. Even the richest people are very unhappy with their lives. In order to be happy you need to

follow your passions and the riches and successes will follow along later.

- There are many ways to look for and find your passion. You can learn what your passion is by asking yourself many questions. You might have the answer decorated all over your house and walls.
- If you have a true passion and you have obstacles stopping you from achieving living the dream then you must get past them and you can. Anyone can be successful with a passion. They can turn it into their own personal business easily if they want to.
- The key ingredient is to believe in your passion that it will work for you and work extremely hard. The harder you work the more successful you will be. If you have a wait time and cannot get started right away you can do initial planning for your goals.
- Remember to always set goals with stepping stones to get to them. You will be able to see the progress you are making toward your goal and know how much longer it will take you. Award your achievements as you meet your milestones and get closer to your goals.
- You are a person who is worth living their passion. You have the same capabilities as anyone else. You deserve to be happy and you deserve to live out your passions.

Chapter 3

Improve your current position now

As I have already stated, having your own business is the only way for you to make real money and to obtain total freedom, but this won't come overnight. Now considering you are in current employment, I suggest that you carry on with this as it would be foolish to stop your income; however, I would at least try to increase the income from your current employment.

Asking for a pay rise

"The quality and quantity of the service you render, plus the attitude with which you render it, determine the amount of pay you get and the sort of job you hold." **Dr Napoleon Hill**

The first thing to do is to be honest with yourself. How much money do you deserve? Look at your own work, your attendance and your contributions. Are you putting sixty-five minutes into an hour or are you just coasting by? Imagine that you were the Chief Executive Officer of the company - would you be happy and delighted with the performance and the service that you provide to the company? If you cannot truthfully say that you are giving your job 110% attention, then you cannot ask for a pay rise until you do.

Those who do no more than they are paid for have no real basis for requesting more pay, because they are already getting all they deserve to earn. You see, you need to deliver the extra benefits to your employer before you can ask for extra pay; some people might say that if they had a pay rise they would work harder, but it doesn't work like that. I remember when I asked for a pay rise in a previous employment - the employer gave testimony to my commitment and hard work and they gave me a pay rise because I asked for it.

If you are totally truthful and you strongly believe that you have an excellent case for a pay rise, then you should challenge your employer for a higher wage. If you are just coasting by then you should be happy with what you're getting and start putting your efforts into your new business.

Preparing a case for a pay rise

It is very important to write down the reasons that you feel you are entitled to a pay rise or a better position. Write a letter stating the facts. Ask for a meeting with the relevant person in your organisation and before the meeting, preferably the night before, use the declaration technique (more details about this in my book *How to occupy till He comes – Self-Development*) and say, 'In Jesus' name I have increased my wage by...' (use a specific amount). Visualise yourself in the meeting with Master Jesus; you are smiling and calm. Visualise yourself being given the pay rise.

On the day of the meeting, stay calm, speak slowly and clearly, sit up straight and demand what you deserve. Hand over a copy of the letter you have prepared and read it out.

IMPORTANT:

Keep your mouth shut and never tell anyone in your organisation, even your closest workmate, what you are doing; whether you get a pay rise or not is between you and your employer. Many employers will be worried that they will now have to give everyone a pay rise, but by keeping quiet about it both before and after, you will be able to eliminate that problem.

The outcome

A yes answer

If the answer is yes, then well done, you have increased your salary; however, don't let your guard down and remember that having your own business is your ultimate goal. It is good that you have increased your salary, but this is still not acceptable so remember to continue with your good work.

A neutral answer

Your employer may argue with you that you are worth more, but they are not able to pay you any extra salary at this time. Now this is where you need to start bargaining, and you should have made a list of things that you will accept other than money, such as: a better job title, attending a training course, extra paid holidays, a better company car, flexible working hours, gym membership and any other benefits that you can think of - even if it's a one-off £100 gift voucher then at least you've walked away with something.

A no answer

It is regrettable that your employer does not see the value of your talents. You haven't lost anything by asking and you are not the loser, your employer is. It is very important to stay calm and either go back to your employer or write a letter stating that you are very disappointed; however, you will continue to work at your best level and you hope that a review could be made in the future. Now you know where you really stand, and just as if the answer had been positive, your ultimate goal is still to aim for your own business.

Summary to raising your salary

If you don't ask, you don't get.

"Ask, and it shall be given you; seek, and ye shall find; knock, and it shall be opened unto you." Matthew 7:7 KJV.

Most companies will not come up to you and say, 'Here's an extra £1,000 a month.' You need to make the first move. Yes it takes courage, but with good preparation and by confessing positively you can do it because, 'You can do all things through Christ who strengthens you.' Whichever way it goes, you are a winner for asking. If you get a pay rise, you win and if you don't, you now know where you stand; at least you have tried and that makes you a winner in my eyes.

Don't make threats which you are not willing to carry out and even if you are willing to carry them out, soften the threat. For example, don't say, 'I am walking out today', say, 'This leaves me in a very difficult position and I will have to consider my options.'

I do know that sometimes our emotions overcome common sense, but please THINK before you say something that you may regret - pause for thought. Wherever possible leave your employer on good terms; it really is a small world and there may come a time when you need to do business with them or ask for a favour in the future.

A point about your current employment

Although I said earlier that it was wise to keep current employment while you're getting started in business, don't make the mistake of feeling too comfortable, for example, 'It doesn't matter if I fail, I've still got my daytime job.' Many people work far better under serious pressure; I had to make it work almost immediately and I did. Now if I had the comfort of another income I may not have achieved this success. If you are reading this and you do not have any current employment you may discover that this is a real blessing. Not having any money coming in scared me into success. I'll talk more about why having too much start-up capital can be DISADVANTAGE; yes, I did say disadvantage! Many people think that throwing money at a problem is the easy solution; however, I know from my own business experience that this is not the case and you can outsmart the larger 'fat cat companies' who have massive budgets.

Chapter 4

Starting your own business

As we have already outlined, you don't want to give up your daytime job just yet, so you will need a business which is flexible, can be run out-of-hours, can be run from home and started on a small budget. At the same time you want a business which can grow and expand with your needs and aspirations.

Now I know of various ways to make money and I could have listed them all here, but most of these businesses have a ceiling; however, I know of one business that is better than all the others and that is the one that I will suggest you go into.

Now this business does divide into two, but the principals are the same for both businesses and I will explain as we go on.

The best business in the world

This business has been around for many years and will continue to thrive. It is truly the last business where the 'little man or woman' can compete with multinationals and beat them.

The business is called DIRECT MAIL/MAIL ORDER/DIRECT MARKETING and there is probably no other business in the world where so many men and women have started from scratch and become millionaires and even billionaires. I could list thousands of names and companies who owe everything to mail order. They include Richard Branson of the Virgin Group, who started selling records via mail order with adverts in student magazines and working from a bedsit. Another person who owes everything to mail order is Anita Roddick of the now worldwide cosmetics and toiletries group The Body Shop. She started by selling a few beauty products and advertising them in teenage magazines. My list can go on and on...

What is so great about mail order?

The lifestyle and riches that mail order/direct marketing can bring are beyond your wildest dreams. With mail order you can choose the hours you work - you can work for three months of the year and then take the rest of the year off. You can work from the comfort of your own home and you can operate in your pyjamas if you want to! You can live anywhere in the country and it can be in the middle of nowhere. Now there may be days when you will be working for 15 hours a day, fulfilling orders, sending out mails, etc. but this should not bother you, because firstly, it's your business and secondly, you're making money. The key to this business is choice, freedom and the fact that there is no ceiling or limit. You can start the business from your kitchen and it can grow like Virgin and The Body Shop into a worldwide business.

What mail order is not

Mail order is not a 'get rich quick' scheme; however, if you get the right product you can make it big very quickly. It is not an opportunity to deceive people and sell shoddy goods. As already mentioned, there will be days when you will work so hard that you'll be wrecked; however, the upside far outweighs the downside. Please do not confuse mail order with multilevel marketing, chain letters or any other type of home business scam that you may have read about. Mail order is a legitimate and well-established business I am proud to be associated with.

What you need to succeed in mail order

What you need is a get-up-and-go personality, a certain amount of self-discipline, determination, a desire to succeed and the wish to start developing all the abilities you know you have inside you, but have never had the opportunity to tap into. In mail order you need the ability to adapt and think quickly. You need to learn new techniques and copy successful formulae. You need to be able to do a bit of everything; one minute you'll be working on your computer, then you'll be answering the phone, then you could be packing goods or sending out a mailshot and then a few hours later you might be researching products and designing adverts. You need to be flexible and willing to do whatever it takes; if you're the only employee and the bin needs emptying or a sack of post needs to be taken to the post office, you can't say, 'It's not my job' or 'It's not my department'- EVERYTHING is your department, especially in the early days.

Hold on, this sounds a bit difficult!

Listen, I never promised you money for nothing. I promised you a legitimate business where you can earn as much as you want and I promised you a business that will give you freedom and a great lifestyle. This business will, however, take some time, effort and hard work. Large amounts of money may come to you very quickly, because when you earn money over a period of time it will TASTE much better than if you inherited it or won the lottery. To succeed in this and any other business you need to really want to be successful. Sure people will say that they believe they can make money from direct mail, but deep down inside they know money doesn't really come that way; they truly believe that they will win their fortune, or they will inherit millions from an unknown, long-lost relative.

Well, many self-made millionaires didn't inherit or win their money; they all made it themselves through their own businesses. One thing I have noticed is that people who succeed in business have a plan. Just like personal goals, they have a plan for their business and they plan for success. Not everyone who has a plan for success achieves success right away, but those who stick to it, and adapt and change their plan to meet the changing conditions in the marketplace, usually succeed.

It is pointless going into business if you think you're not going to make it or that you'll be happy to earn just an extra £200 or £300 a week - it's not worth it. You need to go into business knowing that you will succeed and that you will earn all the money that you deserve. So if you are 100% with me then read on; if you're not then don't bother starting - you'll end up losing the little you have.

Just do it

During this section I will disclose a great deal of information on how to get your business up and running. I have worked very hard to give you as many secrets as I can; however, there is one element that you must do and that's to PUT IN INTO PRACTICE, as quickly as possible. I don't expect you to be able to put all of the information into practice at once and I don't expect you to be perfect; however, I do expect you to start! You see, many people will say, 'I can't start yet, I don't know everything' and while I believe in good research and planning, I also believe in just going for it.

Contrary to popular belief, I believe in starting something badly or in a small way, rather than doing nothing. If you keep putting off starting your business until you know everything about everything, then you will never start.

"Better to do something imperfect than to do nothing flawlessly." R.H. Schuller

That is a fact! I started my business with far less knowledge than you will have after reading this book. Circumstances forced many to start their businesses even though they weren't ready.

Keeping it real

If you want the theory on how business works, then go to the library or a business bookshop and you'll find hundreds of guides on starting your own business. I can truthfully tell you that these books, on the whole, are terrible and the easiest way for your business to fail is to follow these theory books. They are normally written by people who have never made any money in business; they are spectators and they have never played the game.

The information I will disclose to you is as it is today; it is not what the book says should happen, it is what really does happen. If you were going to war, would you want to read a book on how you should fight the war written by a researcher, or would you want to read a book by someone who's just won a war and has had first-hand experience of war, not textbook theories?

Come to war with me, and I'll show you the real secret weapons and facts that you need to know, not the theory.

Now back to business...

What is mail order?

Mail order is supplying goods and sometimes services to clients whom you have never seen and they have never seen you or the product. The initial contact comes through an advert or a sales letter, inviting the customer to buy your product. The customer either phones the order through or returns an order form; you then process the order and send the goods either by mail or in most cases today, by courier.

Today you can purchase almost anything through the mail; this includes books, DVDs, computers, CDs, clothes, toys, furniture, vitamins, loans, keep-fit equipment, food, flowers and just about anything else you can think of. The most important factor that is leading to the explosion in the growth of mail order is the convenience and ease of direct mail shopping. Another big factor is the customer's attitude towards direct mail. Today's shoppers are different and they will buy goods from strangers thousands of miles away. Nearly everyone has a phone and most people now have a credit card.

Imagine 100 years ago - nobody would buy anything via mail order. You would have to go to a local store and buy the product face to face from someone you knew. In many cases you would barter. No one had a phone or credit card and there wasn't a reliable postal service.

The agency/consultancy side of this business

Now here is the second part of this business. The basics and the principles are the same and you will need the same qualities and the same equipment; the only difference in an agency/consultancy business is that there are no direct products - you are more of a middleman. Examples of agency/consultancy businesses are recruitment agencies, advertising agencies, finance agents, IT consultants, etc.

Let's take the example of a recruitment agency - the agency is a middleman between the prospective employee or candidate and the employer. The agency earns a fee from the employer, so unlike a traditional mail order company where you sell a product or book, this time you are selling a service, but the principles are the same.

A consultancy is where you offer your expert advice to companies on your chosen subject. It could be marketing, motivation, advertising, computers, etc. The product in this case is therefore YOU.

Getting started in mail order

The first items that are worth either buying, borrowing or renting, are a computer and a laser printer. The computer does not have to be state of the art. The laser printer should be a Hewlett Packard LaserJet type. If at all possible, have access to broadband, as this will give you a link to the Internet. You will also need a phone and a postal address; again, I will show you how to get a real postal address.

Now, if you have a computer and a Microsoft Word/desktop publisher then that is excellent; however, if you don't, it is crucial to your success that you get one and learn how to use it. You see, I want to show you the EASY way to make money in business. I want to steer you away from all the mistakes that amateurs make. If you want to be successful you have to look successful and this starts with the letters and correspondence that you send. I am afraid that people do judge a book by its cover and in direct mail, your sales letter is your cover.

A good friend of mine is a mail order millionaire in America. When she started out in business her home had just been destroyed by a tornado and she was living in a mobile home. She did not have any indoor plumbing and her phone was fifty yards from the door, attached to a temporary pole. She was living in poverty and yet she had a computer and a laser printer. Why?

Even though she was down and out, her letters and correspondence were perfect and gave the impression that she was a massive corporation working from a big office. Her direct mail offers were convincing and had credibility - after all, no one could see her!

You need to be able to do the same. If I wrote you a sales letter on a scrap piece of paper with stains all over it and using an old typewriter, would you take much notice and would you send me any money?

Now if I wrote to you on a professional piece of letter headed paper with a beautifully formatted letter in a nice font, you would take me seriously. First impressions count and in direct mail you need to make a good impression.

Learning how to use your computer

It is pointless having the best equipment if you don't know how to use it. Take the time to learn the basics of writing a letter and producing documents using a desktop publisher. Luckily the software is very user friendly these days and they come with very good manuals. A point about software: you don't need the most expensive software on the market; in most cases you can buy cheaper versions that do 90% of what the expensive packages do.

Computer training

Most schools and colleges offer evening classes and short courses in computing and if you need help then I suggest that you enrol on a course. It is not important to know everything about computers - you just need to learn the basics so you can produce the results that you need. For example, you probably don't know how a calculator works inside, but you know how to use one and get a result from it and that is the same with a computer.

Buying a computer, software and peripherals

The best way to buy a computer today at the lowest price is through mail order. I have bought all my computers this way and I suggest you get hold of a copy of a magazine called Computer Shopper.

Incorporating a company in the United Kingdom and USA

If you plan to be successful in business, which you do, then I strongly recommend that you set up a Limited Company. The process can be handled by a company registration agent and the whole service should cost no more than £150. A United Kingdom Limited Company requires just one director. You will also need a registered office which is the legal address that any documents will be served to; many companies use the address of their solicitor or accountant but you can of course, use your trading address.

Deciding on a company name

Think very hard about a company name, as you need to give a good impression; however, make sure that the company name is credible and not too long. I have seen names like 'European International Overseas Import and Export Limited' and that is just too long.

Now you will probably want to think of three or four company names, as your choices may already be registered at Companies House. I would also be careful about registering a name that is too similar to another company. Let me explain: it is possible to fool Companies House into registering a name that has already been registered, by adding words such as UK, Company, Direct, etc.

Let me give you an example: if you discovered that 'First United Direct Limited' is already registered, you could register 'First United Direct (UK) Limited' and Companies House will normally allow it - I know because a company did it to me! Now although Companies House will register it, the company that was already registered could easily sue you for this, especially if you are in the same or similar business, so tread carefully when registering your company name.

Why should I set up as a Limited Company when I haven't even started yet?

Well, when you start your business you will need to print stationery, get a telephone line, open a bank account, etc. and by registering a company, you will be ready to give the details that they require.

Now the reasons why I have always traded as a Limited Company are as follows:

a) It gives the impression that you're not a one-man band; people assume that a Limited Company is a real business.

b) A Limited Company provides just that - limited liability. And although legislation has reduced the amount of protection a Limited Company gives you, you are still able to keep your personal assets safe should your company be sued for something or hits trouble.

c) It's easier to sell the business. You are setting this business up to succeed and when you become successful you may decide to sell your business - you could be taken over or you may decide to list on the Stock Exchange. A Limited Company is far easier to sell and value than an unincorporated company, such as a Sole Trader or a Partnership.

d) It is easier to raise money without using your personal assets; money can be raised on the strength of the company's accounts and assets.

e) You can sell shares in your company to equity investors and friends, etc.

Disadvantages:

a) You have to file an annual return, which is public information for a UK company; your company accounts are also available for inspection by anyone who wants to see them at Companies House.

b) Accounting costs are normally higher for a Limited Company, although there are provisions for simplified accounts for smaller companies, which reduce the costs.

c) National Insurance and Taxation is more complex for a Limited Company.

Now I am not a solicitor or an accountant and at the end of the day, the choice is yours as to whether you incorporate. You may also choose to incorporate your company overseas, to take an advantage of possible tax benefits. I have listed two

UK companies and one American company who are reputable, which I have used, and they will be able to send you more details on incorporating a company. I also recommend that you go to your library and take out some books on limited companies and company law.

NOTE FOR USA: It still seems that Delaware has a great deal to offer and I believe that it is still the best state to incorporate in. One of the best US company agents is The Company Corporation in Wilmington, Delaware. I have also read and heard a lot about the different tax advantages of different US companies and I strongly believe that the 'S' corporation is still the best way to incorporate and to protect your personal assets. The Company Corporation publishes various books and leaflets on this subject. Take some time to think about the legal status of your company, i.e. Sole Trader, Partnership or Limited Company. You may wish to ask people you know why they trade as a Sole Trader or Limited Company.

Let me summarise by saying that if you are going to incorporate a Limited Company, make sure that you use a good registration agent and even if you have to pay them a bit more, let them help you with all various legal forms, shareholder certificates, minutes and company seal, etc.

Note: When you form a Limited Company make sure that they incorporate the company from scratch; some agents use ready-made companies and then they file a name change to the company that you wanted - I don't like this practice.

My recommended Company Agents are:

For UK (Ltd, Plc), Channel Islands and tax havens:

Overseas Company Registration Agents Ltd (OCRA)
Companies House
Tower Street
Ramsey, Isle of Man
IM8 1JA
Telephone: 44 1624 811000
Fax: 44 1624 815548
Website: www.ocra.com

Spencer Company Formations
1st Choice Business Solutions
27 Old Gloucester Street
London
WC1N 3AX
Telephone: 44 203 239 5591
Fax: 44 845 330 7292
Website: www.1stchoice-formations.co.uk

For USA:

The Companies Corporation
725 North Market Street
Wilmington, Delaware

19901
USA
Telephone: 1 800 818 6082
Fax: 1 302 636 5440
Outside the US: 001 302 575 0440
Website: www.incorporate.com

Let me add that I am not being paid by any of these companies to recommend them. I found that they provided me with a good service and at reasonable rates in the past, hence I am recommending them. Feel free to do your own research as you may find others that you would prefer to deal with.

Setting up a bank account

You will need a bank account to pay money in and to pay company expenses. A business bank account is totally separate from your personal account. If you are trading as a Limited Company, you are the director of the company and technically an employee, so don't pay any business expenses out of your own account and don't pay your personal bills out of the business account.

Opening a business account is fairly simple and all the banks are desperate for your business, so you will get FREE banking for the first year at least.

Depending on your position with your current bank, you can either open a business account with them, or if you're not on best terms with them, then start afresh with a new bank. I will talk more about banks, accepting credit cards, borrowing money, etc. at a later stage.

If you are trading as a Limited Company the bank will require:

a) Original certificate of incorporation

b) Copy of the memorandum and articles of association

These documents will be given to you by the company registration agent.

Please remember: The bank works for you; they are your servant, not vice versa! As with anyone, treat people who work there in a friendly and courteous manner, whether it's the junior cashier or the senior manager, but expect and demand the highest level of service and respect from them. You should be addressed as Sir or Madam and nothing should be a problem. Just because you are small fry today, it doesn't mean that you won't be a big fish tomorrow. Over time a bank can make a lot of money from you and they should start treating you well from day one.

I will talk later about why the 'little guy' should be treated with respect and give my own personal experiences, but here is a true story that I will always remember:

The late Sir Gordon White, who was the other half of the successful 80s conglomerate, Hanson Trust Plc, went to his bank many years ago. This was when the company was in its early days, as he needed to do some business (I won't mention the bank but they were an American bank).

Gordon White was left waiting in a draughty corridor for over 30 minutes; he wasn't offered any tea or coffee and when he finally saw someone, it was a junior manager who clearly was not qualified to deal with his query. Frustrated with the service, he demanded to see the senior manager and after a further delay, he finally saw a manager. He then asked the manager to confirm what his company's balance was with the bank (the balance was in the millions) and Mr White then replied, "No, that's the balance I did have with your bank!" He closed the account there and then and transferred his money elsewhere.

For over 30 years that bank has tried to get Hanson's business back and they have never succeeded. Just think of the millions that the bank lost in future fees just because of simple courtesy!

On the subject of banks, I don't know why but most people think that they're in business to provide a service to the community or that they are some sort of government body - this is not the case. Banks exist for one reason only and that is to make as much money as they can; they have no morals, feelings or any loyalty to anyone other than the directors and shareholders.

Letter headed paper

To be perceived as a serious business, and that's what you must be seen as, you need a professional letterhead. A letterhead may not seem important to you, but it is the first contact that most of your clients, contacts and customers will have with your company. And if your letterhead does not build confidence in your ability to get the job done, it will cost you business.

Creating a letterhead

I normally design the letterhead myself using my computer and then take the artwork to my printer. If you don't want to design the letterhead yourself, then your local print shop will be able to do this for you and it is normally FREE, as long as you print the paper with them. If you have a friend who is good at art then they could design a logo for you.

Letterhead Rules:

1. The letterhead should have a clean and uncluttered look
2. The font (typeface) should be easy to read, especially the company name, address, telephone number, fax number and email

address/web address. Never use these types of fonts in a letterhead as they are too hard to read and look very bad.

Sample Bad Fonts

- *This is a bad font for business*
- *This is bad font for business*
- THIS IS A BAD FONT FOR BUSINESS

3. Don't make your letterhead look like a rainbow; too many colours do not look good and they end up costing you more money. Use two colours, such as blue and red, or black and green. You can also use tints if you wish.
4. Try and formulate some company colours and a logo, or a typeface style that you can carry throughout your business. Look at what other big companies are using. A one-man/woman business can still have a corporate image.
5. Use white paper (it makes black text stand out better) - normally 100gms or 110gms. You will want the paper to be thicker than normal photocopier paper, but it doesn't have to be so thick that you need a crowbar to fold it with! That is a total waste of money and is what most solicitors use, who charge huge fees.
6. Don't have a raised letterhead; you will find that laser printers do not like it and the heat

from the printer can make it crack (I know because I had raised paper once).

7. Don't forget that if you are a Limited Company you will need to put the company registration number and registered address at the bottom of the paper.

A good letterhead won't be as expensive as you think. Print a small quantity to start with, normally 500, and then take it from there. Shop around for printing prices as there can be big variations; check your Yellow Pages, the Internet, etc. for printers. Now although a cheap quote is vital, don't sacrifice quality for the sake of a few pounds; some back street printers use old machinery that produce awful results.

At this point I must stress that it is very important to build up a good relationship with a printing firm. Depending on how big your business gets and your requirements, you will need a printer who is very flexible, has the latest technology, is able to print in colour and produce brochures, etc.

Business Cards

A business card is an essential item to carry in your wallet or purse. It should have your details on, just like a letterhead, and your name in a clear font with your title underneath, i.e. Managing Director.

A trend at the moment is to print on the back of the card a brief description of what your company does, for example:

Computer Consultancy

Software Programming

Computer Training

Computer Installations

Phone/Fax

You need a dedicated business line and it's easy to get a phone put in. Just make sure that you set the phone up in the name of your company and that the bills are made out to the company.

Normally you will start with one line and one number; try to get an easy number to dial and remember. As well as taking the line I would also recommend that you get caller divert, which will allow you to divert the number to another number. Also caller display, as this will allow you to see the number of the person who is calling you. This is very good for direct mail when taking orders, in case you get cut off. As well as your phone you will probably want a simple answering machine.

Fax machines

I've had a fax machine for many years and I would be lost without one. You can either rent or buy a fax machine. If money is tight, there's nothing wrong with buying a second-hand fax machine - my machine is eight years old and still going strong.

Now here's a big mistake that small companies make: to save the extra line rental they put the phone and fax machine on the same line. This is a BIG MISTAKE, don't do it - it proves that you are a little guy; get a separate line installed for the fax. If you are installing two lines at once, the phone company will normally give you a discount on the second line anyway.

Mailing address

This is a big stumbling block for most home businesses as they don't want to advertise their home address; even if they do, a residential address doesn't look good on a company letterhead. The simple solution is to use a business centre, sometimes known as a services office.

Business centres

A business centre gives you a permanent office address that you can use, but you don't have to have physical space at the office. All your post and messages are held for you and can either be posted on to your home address or preferably you can drop in and collect them.

Business centres offer an excellent service and are ideal for the home business user. Most business centres offer many other services, such as secretarial services, outgoing post handling, faxing, photocopying, etc. You can also hire an office or a boardroom by the day, or in some cases for just half a day, which is excellent if you have meetings and you don't want to hold them at home.

I have listed some UK business centres here and you can also consult your local Yellow Pages or Google them on the Internet. For those that may require an overseas office, then Regus have a network of business centres all over the world.

UK business centres

Regus operates in over 80 cities across the UK, namely: Aberdeen, Belfast, Cardiff, Exeter, Dartford, Farnborough, Gateshead, High Wycombe, St Helier (Jersey), London, Manchester, etc. For your nearest city visit their website.

www.regus.co.uk

Contact a Business Advisor on 0845 300 3585

Worldwide business centres

The Regus Group Network has 1100 Business centres in 85 countries and includes four brands: Regus Business Centres, HQ Global Workplaces, Stratis, and Business Meeting Places. The company provides more than 100,000 clients with flexible and cost-effective workplace options to meet their specific needs. Whether using a fully furnished Regus office, virtual office, meeting room, or video conferencing facility, businesses working with Regus are able to establish an immediate presence at prestigious business centre locations in business hubs and capital cities around the globe. For more details visit their websites:

www.hq.com

www.regus.com

http://www.regus.co.uk/search/global-index.aspx

Contact an International Business Advisor on 0845 300 3586

NOTE: If you have caller divert, you can divert your calls to the business centre when you are out; it is better to have a live person answer your phone rather than an answering machine, especially during office hours.

Accepting credit cards

Today most people have a credit card or at least a debit card. I strongly recommend that you set up merchant facilities to accept Visa, MasterCard, and American Express; also in the UK, Switch/Delta debit cards.

Credit/debit cards make payment very convenient. You must make it as easy as possible for the client to be able to pay you and it is far easier for a client to give you a credit card number than it is to pay by a cheque or postal order.

Now there are a few disadvantages in accepting credit cards: firstly, there is a fee which you have to pay - it's about 4% on credit cards and 70p per transaction on debit cards - regardless of the sale amount; secondly, you are liable for 'Charge Backs', which means that if there is a problem with the credit card you can be forced to give the credit card company the money back.

Now I have accepted credit cards for many years and although you may experience a few fraudulent transactions, on the whole the benefits far outweigh the disadvantages. In mail order you have to be more vigilant than most, as you will be accepting credit cards over the phone, through the post and over the Internet (you will not normally see the actual card); this leaves you open to fraud; however, there are steps that you can take to reduce credit card losses and here are my rules:

1. Authorise every single transaction, whether it is £5 or £5,000. If you have an online terminal then it is easy.

2. When taking an order over the phone, make sure that you take their full address and telephone number. Ask if this is the address that the card is registered to. If you are

suspicious then phone the number back and see who answers the phone; it is possible to tell if it's a phone box because you will normally hear a beeping noise in the background. You can also check with Directory Enquiries to see what number comes up under that name and address.

3. Only ship goods to the address that the card is registered to; never allow the client to send a taxi or their own courier to collect the goods. If the client wants to pick the goods up from you, then make sure that you treat the transaction as a retail transaction, i.e. ask for the credit card, swipe the card and get the client to sign in front of you.

4. Depending on the value of the goods, I suggest that you send them by Recorded Delivery post, so you will have the signature of the recipient. This way if someone phones up claiming they haven't received the goods, you will have proof of the dispatch and who signed for them.

5. Be alert. Watch out for very large orders and watch out for repeat orders very close to each other. Look out for such things as someone ordering five of the same item, especially if it is unlikely that it is a gift item. If in doubt, phone your credit card clearing company and ask for their advice and explain to them what has made you suspicious.

Why you may not be able to get credit card merchant facilities

Firstly, I want to make this very clear: it is a PRIVILEGE to be able to accept credit cards, not a RIGHT. Remember this throughout your negotiations with the bank and you'll get on fine.

The credit card company will be wary of you, especially in the early days, because many banks have suffered huge losses though fraudulent credit card transactions. For example, you get a merchant account, charge up thousands of pounds in orders, you get paid, you don't deliver the goods, you skip town and the credit card company is left with the loss and they have to refund all the cardholders.

Now I hope and expect that everyone reading this is honest and is in the business for the long-term benefits; however, there are people out there who will set up in business to do this and unfortunately, due to these people (most of whom end up getting caught), the rest of us have to suffer.

Proving that you are legitimate

You need to prove that you are legitimate and you are an honest person and have things such as:

1. A good credit rating. If you have defaulted on any loans or credit cards then it won't look good; however, if you can demonstrate that you pay your debts, keep your credit card

payments up to date and you are genuinely trustworthy, then this will help your case.

2. Trade references/personal references. Any evidence which backs up that you are trustworthy. If you know someone in business who accepts cards then maybe they could give you a reference.

3. Show that you are serious about business. A good letterhead, a business phone line, a fax line, a brochure or catalogue, etc. shows that you are not a fly-by-night operation. Also, have some stock to show the bank/credit card representative. Even if you are working from home you can still show that you are serious.

4. Explain to the bank/credit card representative that you offer a full money back guarantee and that any queries that arise will be dealt with promptly. The credit card company wants an easy life; it doesn't want hundreds of customers complaining that they haven't received their goods or that they're not happy with your company. Also offer to indemnify the bank against any credit card problems and explain that you will never take payment from the credit card until you are ready to ship the goods.

You may think that the above seems a little excessive, but believe me it's worth it. I've never seen any other book explain the importance of accepting credit cards, but just ask anyone in the mail order or retail business how crucial credit/debit cards really are.

Borrowing money

I will start by saying that I hate borrowing money and I believe that if you have to borrow to start a business, then it is a bad business.

Fortunately, the businesses that I am going to show you require little start-up capital; therefore you can avoid borrowing money. The only time that I have borrowed any money was for a mortgage on my house. My goal is to own my house outright - that is a goal you should all aim for. To own your house is a great sense of security - if everything goes wrong, you still have somewhere to sleep at night.

Back to borrowing money; I suggest that you use your own savings and try to avoid raising any money from your friends or family, unless you really have to.

Standby credit/credit cards/overdrafts

I have always had, and still have, a few credit cards and access to large amounts of credit, should I ever need it. In the saving money section I will tell you who the best credit card companies are.

I suggest that you do the same and have some credit to fall back on, just in case things don't go as planned or your timing is slightly out. Now only you will know if using credit will make matters worse or will in fact help you out of a temporary problem, for example:

Scenario 1

If things are going badly and your business is genuinely not going as planned, then it would be foolish to start using up credit and running up debts. Throwing money at a problem doesn't cure it.

Scenario 2

Business is genuinely going well; however, due to a few factors that you didn't calculate, you have a temporary shortfall. Now you will know whether it is temporary or not - don't fool yourself. Another scenario would be that a genuine opportunity has come up to buy some stock or equipment at a reduced price, for example at an auction, where payment is required immediately.

In this scenario I would suggest that you use temporary credit; however, my number one goal would now be to pay that debt off as quickly as possible because long-term debts (just like a mortgage or a long-term loan), end up costing you a fortune, but a short-term debt, even if the interest rate looks high, always works out cheaper when you pay it within a few months.

Don't forget that if you buy something on a credit card you can get up to 50 days interest-free credit, which may just be long enough to get you out of your shortfall. This doesn't work on a cash advance, as most credit cards charge interest from Day One.

Another advantage of borrowing on a credit card is that you can pay back variable amounts. For example, you take an advance of £2,000 and the first month you pay back the minimum amount, which is say £100, and the next month you can pay back the whole amount without any penalty.

Now if you were to take out a loan you would be fixed to a payment schedule, i.e. £200 over 60 months, and although you can pay the loan off early, most banks charge early redemption penalties that can be very high.

Overdraft

Never, ever, take out a bank overdraft (either authorised or unauthorised) - it's not worth the hassle. This goes for personal and business accounts and I know that a few banks now offer interest-free overdrafts for small amounts, but don't even use this. If you are going to be short of money in a personal or business bank account then you should raise the money elsewhere to cover the shortfall (a credit card cash advance) and pay the money into the bank.

Always stay in credit with your bank, even if it's only a small amount. I want you to have a good credit rating and standing with your bank. As you can gather, I am not a big fan of borrowing money (and God does not want His children to be borrowers, but lenders), especially from banks, but it's good to use credit cards wisely both for business and personal use. The nice thing about a credit card/cash advance is that it's instant because you already have the credit line; the last thing you want is a meeting with a bank manager or lots of forms to fill in. The only point you have to watch is when you invest any money into your business. Make sure that you account for this as 'cash introduced' or 'loan to the company' and show the money going back out again when the company repays the loan. Your accountant will be able to advise you more on this matter.

My final word on credit cards is that you must be disciplined enough to get the balance back down to zero as soon as possible; paying off the minimum amount month after month is the road to disaster. However, paying off the minimum amount for a month or two and then paying off large chunks or the whole sum thereafter, is a very sensible way to borrow.

NOTE: Never sign a personal guarantee or offer any bank, finance company or supplier any security in the shape of your family home - it's just not worth it.

Summary

If someone had told me everything that I have just disclosed to you when I first started out, I would have paid them at least £5,000, because that's how valuable this information is. Simple things can make a big difference.

Chapter 5

Finding products to sell

Now that you have a computer and the ability to produce quality correspondence, your next step is to look at products that you can sell.

Research

This is one of the most important factors that will either make or break your direct mail business. The biggest mistake that most people make in mail order and retail businesses is that they do little research into the product they are selling and the market they are selling to.

Look at any high street and you will see that new businesses come and go very quickly. The story normally goes like this: Jackie Smith is made redundant and has a few thousand pounds; she opens a shop, gets advice on sorting out tax, business bank account, etc. but forgets the biggest factor: MAKING MONEY BY MAKING SALES. You see, Jackie Smith hasn't done any research; she doesn't know what the market wants, she sells at the wrong price and when she goes broke she puts it down to bad luck!

My advice is to forget about tax and accountants, etc. because if you don't sell anything, you won't have any tax to pay! Make some money by concentrating on your marketing, sell the right product at the right profit margin and you can then hire the best accountant and solicitor later to look after the paperwork.

The market will make or break you

Unless we identify our market first we will end up like Jackie Smith. We need to put the market first and the product second. We need to know how people think, what they want and feel. What people buy today is not the same as ten or even two years ago. What they buy depends on current news, politics and many other things - even the movies. The film *Jurassic Park* has trebled the sales of wooden dinosaur kits at the Natural History Museum; visitors are up and all of a sudden everyone is interested in dinosaurs. You may not be in the dinosaur business, but you should take my point that you need to know what is going on around you. Watching the right programmes on TV is very important.

Gary Halbert, a top marketing guru, was addressing a seminar in the USA. He gave an example of a business which was a hamburger stand. He told the audience that they had a hamburger stand and he had a stand in competition with them. He would allow them any advantages they cared to name, and he only wanted one advantage.

The audience came up with advantages, such as the best meat, the best position, the biggest stand, etc. Gary said that they could have all those things. All he wanted was one advantage which they hadn't mentioned and he would beat them easily.

"What can it be?" they asked.

"Easy!" said Gary. "The only advantage I need is a HUNGRY CROWD!"

You see, the whole point of this story is the word 'HUNGRY'. Vast fortunes have been lost and many companies have gone broke because the products they sold were not wanted. No one was hungry for them. Of course, with enough time and money you can use the media, press and television to convince people that they need something. Take the example of deodorant: it took over twenty years and literally millions to convince people that they must have it. You and I simply don't have the time and budget to convince people that they want something.

Picking the easy targets

Unlike most people, I am not in the business of reinventing the wheel - I don't care if I am the first to think of a business. In most cases I would prefer to be second or third. What you want and what you should be looking for are easy targets: markets that are desperate for what you are selling - they must be 'HUNGRY'.

The biggest mistake that nearly all companies make is that they spend too much time and money developing a product and then they say, "Who shall I sell this to?" Sounds obvious, so why do most companies do it?

Instead of going to your market and saying, "This is what I have for sale, do you want to buy it?", you should be able to go to your market and say, "Here's your chance to get the product you've desperately been looking for."

Having exactly what the market wants is a sure way to achieve success in business. If you want to buy a car and I try to sell you a boat, it's going to be very difficult for me to sell you a boat.

People buy what they want and not always what they need

Before I go on, I want you to remember that people buy what they WANT and not what they need. Let me give you an example: my friend, who is a successful businesswoman, recently purchased a new Mercedes SL sports car with all the extras. Her previous car was nice enough and got her from A to B in comfort so she didn't really NEED a Mercedes, she just WANTED one.

Let me give you another example: most people NEED life insurance and health insurance, but they don't have it. Why not? Because they don't want to think about death or illness and that is why life insurance is so hard to sell.

In the next few pages I will give you products and specific markets that you can sell to. Before I give you these opportunities on a golden platter, I want to teach you how to fish.

How to fish

If you were starving and I gave you a few fish, you would eat for a few days, but if you were starving and I gave you a fishing rod and taught you how to fish, you would eat forever!

So although I will give you specific opportunities that are available, I will also show you how to look for new ones.

How to find out what people are buying and what they want

Where to start your research

A large newsagent (WHSmith in the UK) is a good place to start. Look at the magazine racks and see which topics have the biggest space. If you go to a large newsagent at the moment, you will see that the following sections are the biggest:

1. Women's magazines and related interests
2. Magazines relating to cars
3. Computers
4. Money/investments
5. Adult titles (I will not advise and encourage any child of God to go into the pornographic business)

A new trend is men's fashion and lifestyle magazines. From my investigations these five topics were taking up more shelf space than any other topic. I have also spotted a big trend in hobby magazines, such as HobbyCraft Magazine, and new men's magazines, such as GQ, Maxim, Esquire, Men's Fitness, etc.

So what does this mean? That there is a market and interest in these subjects. People want to know about them and are willing to spend money on buying these magazines. If they didn't, then the magazines wouldn't be there.

Another way to find out what people are interested in is to go to a bookshop or look at the weekly book charts that show which books are selling the best. Looking through the non-fiction book chart will give you a very good idea of what people are desperate to know more about. A bookshop will also reveal what the most popular selling titles are by the amount of space given to a subject. From my recent investigations at an average bookshop, I saw a large amount of book space given to travel and computers.

Tip: Don't go to a specialist bookshop, i.e. a business bookshop, as this will give you a false impression. Another good way to find out what people are buying is to watch QVC, the shopping channel; also, look for the infomercials on

Sell-A-Vision and tune into late night satellite TV channels. If you're watching QVC and you see that eight hours of their programming schedule is designated to home and leisure, then you know that this is selling well.

How to find millions of mail order buyers

Today names, addresses, purchasing behaviour and other general information is bought and sold quite freely. If, for example, you purchase something from a catalogue, subscribe to a magazine, fill in a competition entry, return a guarantee form and so on, then this will be registered on a mailing list. In the UK there is a book called BRAD Direct Marketing; in the USA it is called SRDS. This book contains about every mailing list there is in the UK. You should be able to get a copy from larger reference libraries. A copy of BRAD currently costs £85 and is worth buying.

BRAD, which stands for British Rate and Data, can be contacted at:

BRAD
Emap Media
33-39 Bowling Green Lane
London
EC1R 0DA
Tel: 0207 505 8246
Fax: 0207 505 8264

NOTE: It is BRAD Direct Marketing that you need for mailing lists because there is also another publication, which is the BRAD that lists all the newspapers and magazines. Just by looking at these lists I can get an instant idea of the size of a market and their profiles. Let me give you an example: there are two lists; one list contains women's dress sizes 12-14 and the other list is women's dress sizes 8-10. From the listed entries I can see that there are around 500,000 size 8-10 names and addresses and over 2 million size 12-14. So if I am going to sell dresses, I would make sure that I cover the 12-14 size, as that is where the main market is.

Renting names

As you can see from the sample BRAD entry page, the details of the list broker/owner are listed. You would contact them and they would supply you with the names and addresses on a disk or on sticky labels. List brokers will also provide you with more detailed information about the list, including how many new names are being added monthly.

The newest way to research and find information for FREE

I have used the Internet and newsgroups for some time now and I am starting to realise that it's a very powerful research and information tool. The best point about the Internet is that I can access it at any time from the comfort of my home, even from my iPhone. In the next few pages I want to explain why you should have access to the Internet. I will keep it as brief and as non-technical as possible.

Dial-up Internet Connections

The fundamental difference between dial-up and broadband Internet connections is the manner in which the connection is made from your PC to the Internet. A dial-up service connects to the Internet through your phone line. The modem in your PC 'calls' an Internet Service Provider (ISP) and connects with a maximum speed of 56,000 bytes per second, better known as a 56K speed connection. Each time your PC dials into the ISP, it is assigned an Internet Protocol (IP) address, which you can think of as an 'Internet address'. A different, unique IP address is assigned at the beginning of each visit so that the ISP can recognise your PC and make sure you can send and receive email, surf the Internet, and so on; basically, this address lets your ISP know where to send the information you are requesting through your modem. In terms of hackers, in order for someone to gain access to your computer, it would be necessary for them to know your IP to successfully do so. The fact that your IP address constantly changes essentially makes your Internet connection more secure.

Broadband Internet Connection

In contrast, when you connect to the Internet via a broadband Internet connection, the process is slightly different. Once your PC is connected to the ISP through a cable or DSL connection, it remains connected until the cable box is disconnected or physically unplugged.

1. Research, information and market testing

Whether you are looking for new business ideas or if you want to find information on your current business, the Internet is a cheap place to start. Imagine that you are writing a newsletter or booklet on tropical plants and you need some more information for this month's issue. With a few searches on the internet you will find pages of information and photos. The scope in which to convert information found on the internet into manuals and 'how to' guides is massive.

2. Email

Email is far cheaper than sending a fax, letter, or using a courier. Once you have an Internet account you can send letters, photos, video clips and sound clips to anyone worldwide, instantly.

Example:

A 10g document to USA is 87p

A 20g document to USA is £1.28

An International fax to anywhere is £1

DHL Courier of 1kg parcel to Europe and the US (average of two days) is £38.95

Email is almost instantaneous.

3. Lead generation, promotional material and direct sales

The internet is one of the most cost-effective ways to distribute sales and generate leads. According to the latest Nielsen Global Online Survey, more than 85% of the world's online population has used the internet to make a purchase - this is about 875 million, up 40% in the last two years. This trend continues to grow steadily every year, a trend that anybody thinking of internet marketing should not ignore. We will discuss online marketing in great details later on in this book.

4. Newsgroups and chat areas

Contrary to what the media makes out, not all chat areas are sex related. There are chat areas on law, sports, computers, business, stocks and shares, etc. A chat area allows you to ask questions, send replies to other members, or just read other people's questions and replies. An interesting chat area I use is in the stock and shares area. Here you can ask a question and normally within 20 minutes someone will give you the answer. For example, XYZ company's shares have fallen sharply today for no apparent reason. I can post the question 'Anyone know why XYZ shares are falling today?' and I would receive an answer shortly.

Summary

According to figures from the Office of National Statistics, in 2008, some 16 million households in the UK had Internet access of some form, with 56 per cent of all UK households having a broadband connection. Compare this with 2006, when approximately 14 million UK homes had access to the Web, and an estimated 15.3 million homes had access in 2007 - the figures speak for themselves; each year more and more people are turning on to broadband.

With advances in telephone technology meaning that more and more customers are now able to make cheaper long-distance calls over the Internet and to access the Internet both out of and in the home, more and more broadband suppliers are offering deals for cheaper mobile and landline phone rates combined with broadband Internet packages.

As this technological convergence continues, providers are increasingly extending their operations into other markets in order to cater for the needs of an ever-expanding market area. Today's broadband market is well furnished with a multitude of providers offering broadband access alongside a variety of extra services.

Choosing the best deals on broadband

There are a few free comparison websites where you can get the best deal by comparing broadband tariffs from different companies at the same time under one website for your convenience. This helps you immensely by saving you valuable time and money. Some of them include the following:

www.moneysupermarket.com
www.simplifydigital.co.uk
www.homephonechoices.co.uk
www.comparethemarket.com/compare-home-phone/
www.uswitch.com/broadband/compare/broadband_and_home_phone/

Chapter 6

The ideal mail order product

The ideal mail order product should be fairly small, lightweight (posting an elephant is expensive), not too fragile, and the product should normally not be available in local stores; most importantly the product must have a high perceived value and offer at least a 200% markup and in most cases a typical 500% markup.

Now let's look at that pricing. A lesson that I learned very quickly in mail order is that selling your product too cheaply is always worse than selling it for too much. It is the mistake that most new businesses make; they think that because they are new in business they should work on small margins. This is not the case.

Let me give you an example: God forbid you needed a heart operation but if you needed a heart operation and there were two doctors - one quotes you £250 all inclusive, and the other quotes you £3,000. Which one would you trust?

I know I would go for the most expensive one; you see price and quality have a psychological connection - it's cheap so it must be rubbish!

Now I am not saying that you should sell a paper clip for £500, and don't think that you'll get away with it either. You still need to ensure that your customer is happy and that they believe they have received more than good value for money. You can always go down in price, but it is very hard to increase a price. For example, let's say that I am selling a new home study course. You enquire and I send you my sales letter - my selling price is £97.77. Now let's say that you haven't responded to the offer after a few weeks. I can then write to you again with a new sales letter and I could offer you a special LAST CHANCE offer of £67.77.

Selling products that you like

I feel that it is important to enjoy and understand the product that you are selling. It is very hard to be enthusiastic about a product which you don't like, for instance, I personally would not sell gardening and DIY items.

Remember that you could be spending 12 or 14 hours a day working, so make sure that you like what you are doing. Now at the same time, I must warn you about selling products just because you like them - they might not have good profit margins or a big market. Your hobbies do not always make good businesses.

Specific products

Some of the best mail order products are:

Information products

This includes books, 'how to' manuals, correspondence courses, self-improvement courses, newsletters, DVDs (training/seminars), spoken word cassettes (self-improvement/spoken books) and computer software peripherals.

Information booklets, 'how to' guides and manuals

People pay good money for information. I have seen a four-page document for £50. Now the ink and the paper would have cost less than £1, but the value was of course the information on the paper. Information that currently sells well includes topics on how to make money, health/fitness, relationships, money saving tips, computers, hobbies/crafts, etc.

Producing a 'how to' manual

You have 3 choices:

1. You can write and research the manual yourself. For example, let's say the topic you have chosen is 'How to make money'. You can research the manual by collating information from the Internet, newspapers, other books, and by interviewing people, etc. and format it yourself using your computer.
2. You can pay a researcher to find out the information and produce you a script.
3. You can find a manual on the subject and purchase the reprint and resale rights, or you can enter into a wholesale agreement to buy the manuals.

Audio information

Anything written on paper can be put on to an audio tape. Today's time-starved consumers are willing to pay for information on tapes and the success of books on tape proves this. Audio information can also be put together very cheaply. An audio cassette costs around 50p and the original master, including using a professional voice-over artist, will cost no more than £300 to £400.

Videos

The videos that I am talking about here are very low-tech information videos, not big budget feature films. There are some things that are easier to explain by showing people in real life, rather than in writing.

Let me give you an example: A friend of a friend in America runs a company that cleans computers and offers other maintenance services to companies. The market for this is very large and so she decided to make a low budget video, showing people what she did and how they could start their own business doing the same thing. All she did was set up a desk in her own house with a computer on it and demonstrated how she cleaned computers. She also went on to explain how she markets her business and what she charges, etc. Her video was made with the help of a friend as the cameraman and a home video camera. To go with the video, she produced a short 'how to' manual and workbook. The manual and the video cost her only US$10 to produce and ship, which is around £7, and she sells the course for US$127 (£90). The last time I heard about this lady, she has sold over 15,000 copies of this video, via mail order. Now in case you're not too good with mathematics, that's over 1.9 million dollars!

Simple ideas like this work. Notice the high profit margin and how by only selling 15,000 she managed to make so much money. Now if she was working on a smaller profit margin, i.e. she sold the package for $39, she would have had to sell over 45,000 to make the same amount.

Another way to make money with videos is by recording trade shows and seminars/conferences. You see, for every one person that attends a seminar/trade show, there are probably ten others that couldn't make it, or didn't want to spend a large amount of money attending the seminar.

Example: Let's say that there is a national seminar for doctors and it costs £300 to attend. Now you could arrange to video that seminar and sell it to the list of doctors who didn't attend for £40 to £60. You can even sell it to those who did attend!

Getting video tape produced

Videos do cost more than audio CDs; however, they also sell for more. For a very simple video, you could produce it yourself at home using a video camera. For seminars you'll probably need two video cameras, extra lighting and a professional microphone.

Editing

Once you have your footage you will want to edit it, add some titles, fades and music etc. A studio will normally charge £70 an hour, which includes an operator. After the various chopping you will end up with a master tape; this is what you make the copies from. Before you go into a studio, be prepared, because studio time goes past very quickly and before you know it you've spent a lot of money.

Have a plan ready of what you want to do, have titles ready on paper, or produce them yourself on your computer and bring them in on a disk.

A video tape costs around £2 for 30 minutes and around £2.50 for 60 minutes. This includes the blank tape and the actual copying. Prices vary and can be reduced significantly depending on volume. Again, just like printing, price is important but so is the quality; badly copied DVDs look very bad.

You can also print inlay sleeves for your video and put it in a professional video case, which cost around 40p each.

More about producing videos

There are various books on producing videos and there is also quite a bit of information on the Internet about this subject. There are even videos on how to produce videos! If you are serious about this, I would recommend going on a short course; various companies advertise these in the back of video magazines.

Buying the rights to a video

Nowadays, it is easy to buy the rights to videos, edit, repackage and sell them. Anyone reading this could buy the rights to a video and do the same. Most of the videos I own are 'How to' videos, which I package together with workbooks, paperwork, etc.

How to buy the rights to a video

The first step is to get hold of a copy of the video and the sales letter. Identify the market that you think would be interested in the video. Look at ways in which you can improve the video, what you could add to the video, i.e. a workbook, help sheets, or a computer disk. What do you think of the title? Could you improve the title name and make it more marketable?

Once you have decided that you can sell the video, then you need to write or phone up the copyright holder and explain what you want to do and how it will benefit him. You could either make a one-off offer for the UK rights, such as US$1,000, or you could offer a small advance of, say US$250, and a percentage of the sales, say 5% of the sale price on each video.

You see the chances are that Joe Smith, the copyright holder, has never even thought about selling the video outside his country, and by you selling the video in the UK then he's got nothing to lose - it's BONUS money to him.

If the copyright holder is in the same country as you, you can still buy the rights; I know that there are many saleable videos that are just sitting on shelves collecting dust. Contact the copyright holder and make a reasonable offer - you'll be surprised how many will agree to your offer.

Newsletters

A newsletter or small magazine is a very good way to get into the media business, with little or no up front costs. Most people are totally unaware of the vast profits and multi-billion pound empires that have been built through the publishing of books, newspapers, magazines and newsletters. Some of the richest people in the world have made their fortunes through owning media companies, including television and radio. Unfortunately, unless you have millions to invest in buying a television/radio station or a newspaper, there are no opportunities for the small businessman/woman to get into the profitable publishing and media industry, except by publishing a newsletter or small magazine.

What is a newsletter and why do people pay for them?

Information is now one of society's biggest needs and most valuable commodities. People will pay large sums of money to find out more about a particular subject. Whereas newspapers, and to a certain extent a magazine, provide a broad overview of a subject, a newsletter would provide very specific information on a particular subject.

Unlike most other forms of media, newsletters can be set up on a very low budget and produce staggering results. Let's say that you have 2,000 subscribers to a newsletter, each paying £40 a year, that's £80,000 a year! The costs of running a newsletter are very low, in fact an eight-page newsletter can be produced, printed and posted for less than £1 per month.

The big advantages of a newsletter are:

1. It can be started from your home.
2. A computer and a laser printer are the only tools you need.
3. You get paid up front. For example, I sell you a 12 month subscription and you pay me now, but I don't have to deliver the newsletters all at once, so technically I am getting an interest-free loan from the subscribers.
4. You have a residual value. Depending on how good your newsletter is you will get renewals, so after 12 months your income doesn't stop, it keeps going! A good newsletter should get around 80% renewals.
5. You can sell your newsletter business when you've had enough, for a substantial amount.

6. There are numerous extra ways to make money on top of subscriptions, including renting out your mailing list, carrying loose inserts and reader's offers, etc.

Let me give you some examples of successful newsletters:

Competitors Companion

This newsletter has over 150,000 subscribers, all paying on average £45 a year. 150,000 X £45 = 6.75 million pounds! Now even after running costs, such as printing and stamps, the newsletter still makes over 6 million pounds a year pre-tax.

So what is this newsletter all about? It's very simple - every month they publish all the new competitions that are open in the UK.

The sort of information they give includes:

- Where to get entry forms from.
- What the competition restrictions are and if any proof of product purchase is required, i.e. three tokens from the side of a packet.
- What the prizes are.
- The closing dates.
- Help with answers.
- Sample competition slogans and tie-breakers.
- Any other news the competitors need.

What a simple idea! The information is always changing and the information is free (they just have a few researchers who track down all the competitions). With the public's massive appetite for winning competitions, this newsletter will continue to grow.

Government Auction News

This is basically a monthly newsletter on where all the various auctions are to be held, what type of goods are available, and general buying advice.

Other successful newsletters are:

Discount travel newsletters
Health and medical newsletters*
Finance and investments newsletters*
Food and wine newsletters
Computer newsletters
Accountancy and taxation newsletters*
Classic car newsletters
Model railway newsletters
Gardening newsletters
DIY newsletters

***Note**

Any newsletter that relates to medical advice must be written by a suitably qualified person. Take legal advice before proceeding.

Investment newsletters are regulated in the UK by the Financial Services Authority (FSA) and again, must be written by a suitably qualified person.

Why everyone in business should publish their own newsletter

I strongly advise that everyone reading this should publish a newsletter, whatever business you are in - even if you give the newsletter away for FREE you will benefit greatly from it. Now I know you are thinking, is this girl serious? Why would I give my customers a FREE newsletter? How do I make any money?

How to make money with a FREE newsletter

Making money by giving something away FREE!

There are many regional newspapers in the UK that are distributed for free, eg The Metro, The Evening Standard, etc. The advertising revenue of course pays for the printing, distribution and staff wages. Many of these newspapers are of good quality and make very good profits.

In England, the ITV, Channel 4 and Channel 5 television channels are free. Their massive overheads are paid for by the commercials.

Can a free newsletter work?

On advertising alone it can be difficult to make your newsletter profitable, but with a combination of reader offers and selling your own goods, it can be very profitable. Unlike a paid-for newsletter, you can sell more advertisements and try to sell a bit harder to the subscriber, as they haven't paid for the newsletter.

Giving a newsletter away free to existing customers

Let's say that we own a computer software company and Joe Smith buys our latest program; instead of forgetting about him as we have now had his money, wouldn't it be a nice touch to offer him 12 months' free subscription to our computer newsletter?

In this newsletter we would have:

- General computer news.
- Updates about the software that he has just bought.
- Hints and tips.
- Details of our other products that we have to sell, including upgrades.

You will sell more software to Joe Smith by sending him a free newsletter every month, rather than sending a sales letter.

So that is how you make money with a free newsletter; remember that a newsletter doesn't cost that much to produce and send out. If it's a free newsletter you don't have to send one out every month - it could be quarterly. Your newsletter can also be literally one or two A4 sheets.

Keeping in regular contact with your customers is very important. Most companies take your money and forget about you, yet if they only sent you a newsletter or a catalogue on a regular basis, the chances are they would get more sales from you and they would be able to create goodwill and a good impression.

NOTE: The firm of accountants that I use now has its own newsletter, which contains all the latest tax news and is sent out to clients free of charge, on a regular basis. This creates goodwill, keeps their customers informed and keeps their name to the forefront.

How do you make a newsletter a winner?

There is one thing that will make or break a newsletter and that is the topic. Pick the right topic and everything else will fall into place. Remember what we said earlier about 'the hungry crowd', well that's what you need for a newsletter. It doesn't have to be a massive crowd, but there needs to be one.

The other thing that you need to concentrate on is marketing your newsletter; in fact, 90% of your efforts will go into marketing the newsletter and the other 10% will go into writing the newsletter.

Summary

A newsletter is a very profitable home business, which can be started with little up front money. A newsletter is also an ideal product that can be sold alongside your existing profession/job.

Computer software/peripherals

There is no disputing that the computer age is here to stay. The first thing that I would recommend is to get a computer and a copy of some software. As I write, one of the richest men in the world is Bill Gates, the founder of Microsoft. This company went from nothing in 1980 to the biggest software company in the world.

Computer software is a fast-changing market and sells very well as a direct mail product. If you decide to sell software, then you have the same three options as if you were selling a book or 'how to' manual:

1. You could write the software yourself if you have the skills and are that way inclined; however, this could take you a lifetime.

2. Find someone else to write the program, or find a program that someone has already written and offer to buy it or license it.

There are many talented programmers and some excellent pieces of software; however, 99% of programmers haven't got a clue about business or marketing, therefore in most cases, these programmers are totally broke. They have great products but they don't know how to sell them, and that's where you come in. Bill Gates is not a billionaire because he's a good software programmer, it's because he is a good marketer. I read that for every programmer that Microsoft employs, they have about ten people in sales and marketing.

As already mentioned, Bill Gates is one of the richest men in the world and the program that started his career was MS-DOS, but the amazing fact that most people don't know is that Microsoft never wrote DOS - it was bought from someone else for a few thousand dollars! Microsoft then licensed the program to IBM and the rest is history. So if Bill Gates can do it so can you - find a good programmer and get them to write the program.

3. Purchase the software from wholesalers /publishers. You can buy software wholesale or direct from the publisher. Software carries a good profit margin; normally a program that retails for £40 can be bought for around £15 or less, depending on quantities.

You can also import software from overseas, normally America. I have a friend that distributed a very good CD-ROM compilation in the UK which he imported from America. The software cost around US$5 (£3) a piece, including shipping and taxes, and he sold it for around £20 retail and £10 wholesale, which is a very good markup.

Peripherals (extra)

These are the extra add-on pieces to a computer, such as computer speakers, sound cards, extra memory, scanners, modems, memory backup drivers, etc.

I have read about the owner of a successful company which sells peripherals in the UK. He regularly goes to the large computer trade shows in Hanover, Germany, such as CeBIT and Computex in Taipei Taiwan, looking for the latest add-ons and imports them over to the UK.

Don't get involved in selling computer hardware

I strongly advise you against selling mail order computers - it is a very competitive market and is best left to the big companies. The margins are far better on software and peripherals and you don't need much start-up capital to start selling software and peripherals; in most cases you only need to order a small amount of stock, then you can place orders only as and when you receive your orders.

Novelty items, kitchen gadgets, health & fitness, jewellery and personalised items

One of the best salesmen/direct marketers in recent years has to be Ron Popeil, better known as Ronco. His products include many kitchen gadgets and time-saving devices. His top tip in direct marketing is to make sure that the product can be sold as a gift. Without Christmas, Mother's Day, Father's Day, birthdays, weddings and so on, most retail stores would go broke! I recommend getting hold of his book *The Salesman of the Century*. In this book Ron Popeil explains how he went from selling kitchen products on a market stall to being one of the biggest direct advertisers in America. Details are listed at the back of this book and anyone who is interested in promoting their products through infomercials or on home shopping channels should definitely read this book.

Products and information that solve people's problems

It seems that most people today have so many problems. As a direct marketer, any products, guides or services that can help to solve problems are very big sellers. You see, if you have a product which solves a common problem, the customer will not even think about the price. Let me give you a few examples of problem solving products:

The problem: Chopping food and preparing vegetables can be difficult and time-consuming.

The solution: The Chop-O-Matic. It cuts and slices food thinly in just seconds, with no mess.

The problem: Back pains

The solution: A massager which straps to your chair and vibrates. The ideal gift for someone you know who suffers from back pains.

Packaging products together

This is a very simple way to make a new mail order product out of existing items. Let me give you a true example that went from being a wacky idea to a very big Christmas seller. The product is Christmas stockings for cats and dogs. For years confectionery manufacturers realised that you could take a few bars of confectionery, put them together in a pretty box or stocking and stick an extra 50% on to the price. The idea came from the USA and now animal lovers in England and Europe are buying them by the millions. All you need is a cheap Christmas stocking and some small dog or cat treats, toys, balls, etc. Many of the goods in the stockings are samples/trial sizes, which can be obtained from the manufacturers for nothing!

Put a nice printed card at the top of the stocking with a picture of a cat/dog and a name tag, so that you can write: To Tiddles, and you then have a finished product. So by taking existing products and putting them together you have made a new product.

Another very successful packaging concept was the introduction of compilation records, tapes, CDs and now mp3s. This was pioneered by a Canadian company called K-Tel in 1970 and later Ronco. Now you have Telstar, Sounds Direct and numerous others. These companies would approach the record companies and pay them a set price and a royalty, based on the hit status of the song. The songs were then put onto a tape or CD and sold on; in the old days, mainly directly through TV and radio.

This concept can be copied for many other products - the computer software CD-ROM that I mentioned was a compilation.

Importing products and ideas

What do the following products and services have in common: jeans, t-shirts, pizzas, pasta, popcorn, shell suits, home delivery of fast food, tool hire, karaoke and dancing cola cans/flowers?

They were all ideas and products that came to the UK from America or other countries. The opportunity to import ideas and products from overseas is enormous. Whenever I go away I'm always looking at possible new products to bring back. It can also work the other way. The Americans love things connected to the British Royal family; they like fine English teas, Scottish shortbread biscuits, etc.

Summary

To summarise, you need to find products and services that people want. You need products that can easily be shipped. You need products which have big profit margins and a high perceived value. If you follow the guidelines that I have given you, I don't think you'll have any problems in finding successful mail order products.

A NOTE ON STOCK: Go easy, especially in the early days, on buying stock; you will probably have to hold a small amount of stock before some newspapers will let you advertise, but you don't want to be left with thousands of books, videos, etc. The key is to have some stock and a good supplier, so that if you receive thousands of orders you can obtain more stock within 7 to 14 days.

Adding value

A large box gives the impression of more value. As previously mentioned, never get into price wars in business - the only winner is normally the consumer and not you. Pricing higher is better than pricing lower; however, a good trick is to add value to your product.

Let's say that you are selling a set of kitchen knives. To add value you could add a cookbook or a guide on how to use the different knives to their best effect; you could also throw in a few other small kitchen gadgets. So even though your price may be slightly higher, you are giving more value.

I deal with a company in America and whenever you order stock, they always throw a few extra bits in the box like a newsletter, brochures, a mug and even a baseball cap!

How to secure products

Most people will not want to invent and manufacture their own products, especially if they are new to mail order. The best way is to source a product through a wholesaler, directly from the manufacturers, or if it's a book or video, from the publisher/author.

The best starting point is to obtain a copy of the book, video or product that you are interested in selling and this way you can get the name and address of the publisher or manufacturer.

The second step is to write them a good letter on your official letter headed paper, explain what your company does and that you would be interested in selling the XYZ product. In the letter you need to demonstrate that you are serious but at the same time, be truthful.

Now we both know that you are just starting out and this could possibly be the first product that you've ever tried to sell; however, there is nothing wrong with writing in your letter 'We are a dynamic, young company which specialises in marketing products such as ... and from our initial research, we believe that we will be able to sell a substantial amount of units.'

I would also state in your letter that you are happy to place an initial test order of 50 or 100 units, depending on the price, and that you are happy to pay for these immediately. You see, if I received a letter like this I would take note - sure you're not a big retail chain, but you have already offered to make a small order and you've offered to pay for the goods on delivery.

This format will work in nearly all cases. The above scenario takes into account that you will be dispatching the product; now in some cases it could be possible for the manufacturer or their dispatch agent to handle your orders; the only downside to this is that you lose some control and you are then disclosing the names and addresses of your customers to the manufacturer.

An easy way to find good ideas for products

An easy way is to 'follow the leader' - watch what other successful mail order companies are doing. An important tip is to get on as many mailing lists as you can; you need to get all those little mail order catalogues and see what they are selling. Watch for the mail order products that are being repeated over and over again.

There is one product that is everywhere. It's a fitness product which gives you a flatter stomach by toning your abdominal muscles. There are many variations, but the principles are the same and their names are all very similar: AB FLEX, AB CRUNCH, AB ROLLER, etc., all of which, I better add, are registered trademarks. By the time you read this you will have purchased one - I have!

My favourite mail order catalogue is:

Shop Direct Home Shopping Limited
1st Floor, Skyways House, Speke Road, Speke, Liverpool L70 1AB
Tel: 08448222321
Website: www.very.co.uk

This catalogue will give you some great ideas for mail order products and will also show you how a good catalogue should be laid out. The best point about this and other catalogues is that they are FREE; it's unbelievable that you are getting ideas for products and examples of advertising copy and it costs you nothing.

A note on copyright and copying others

There is a very thin line between getting ideas and learning from other people and STEALING their ideas. If you take a book and copy it word for word, or if you illegally duplicate a video that you don't have the rights to, then that is STEALING - there is no other word for it. Don't do it because it's not worth it; you may get sued or even have a nasty visit from someone! Believe me, it's been done, especially in the music and video business.

Be a smart copycat

A smart copycat reads a book or an advert, gets ideas, and formulates a plan from other people's work. They then write their own book or produce their own video along similar lines. Nobody can copyright ideas or generic words like 'AT LAST' or 'HOW TO'. Take for instance the supermarket's own brands - their products are so similar to the brand leaders; sometimes the packaging even looks similar. However, as long as the 'own brands' do not purport to be the actual brand, then there is nothing that the brand leaders can do.

Don't forget that you can be a legal copycat if you buy the rights to a product or buy it wholesale. Improving other people's ideas with a superior product, advertising campaign or creating a more appealing package, can be a very quick route to success and it is completely moral and ethical.

A very important lesson

I mentioned earlier about the bank that lost the Hanson Trust account - well you need to remember this. When you make it big one day, which I'm sure you will, and a little guy writes to you asking to buy 50 or 100 units of your product, ALWAYS do business with them and treat them fairly and with respect. Treat them as if they are the biggest chain store in the world and they are placing an order for a million units. Why this great treatment? Because firstly, you don't know who that little guy is. He could in fact be a very big guy, but is just testing the market, and secondly, one day that company working in a studio flat could become the biggest corporation in the world and they will remember you and it will be to your benefit.

I read a true story about a 'little guy' that started producing and selling videos some years ago and he needed to make ten copies of a video. He was new to the business and phoned a few companies from the Yellow Pages; most were not very polite to him or that bothered, and others tried to rip him off on the pricing because he was only ordering a few copies and he was a 'little guy' in the video business. What they didn't know was that he was already a big guy in publishing and he was regularly ordering 10,000 audio tapes at a time. Anyway, one company was polite enough and they offered to copy the ten videos at a fair price and turn them around as soon as they could find a gap in their duplication schedule. The company is still the company that he uses today for duplication and copying; that 'little guy' who started with a ten video order went on to duplicate over 300,000 videos plus, possibly more by the time you read this. Now just think of all those people who wouldn't deal with him for an order of ten - had they done business with him, they would have had a very big customer.

Let me add something else about people in business, especially those who have built up a business from scratch and have climbed up the ladder: THEY HAVE LONG MEMORIES AND THEY ARE VERY LOYAL.

Chapter 7

Advertising and marketing

What we have up to now is nothing without advertising and marketing. You can have the best product, the best piece of letter headed paper, a good address, etc. but if you don't know how to advertise and market your product or service cost effectively, then you will fail and go broke.

I just cannot stress how important this subject is - if you can imagine that a successful business is a cake, then this is 90% of the cake. Let me tell you the facts of life: The best product does not always win; it's the best marketed product that wins; it's the product that the market likes the most that wins.

Let me give you some examples: Some years ago there was a rivalry between the two standard video companies, VHS and BETAMAX. Now anyone who is technically minded will know that BETAMAX was the better product and in fact, is still used in the TV industry; however, VHS won the consumer market - they gained the support and they won the marketing race.

Promoting your product

Let's say that we have done our research and we have negotiated the rights to a product (i.e. the cleaning of a computer video). We now need to write a winning advert and response pack to sell our product. Trying to sell a product without advertising is like smiling in the dark - you know you're doing it, but no one else does! Good advertising will normally sell an inferior product, but bad advertising will always make a good product fail.

There are two ways to advertise and I will show you both:

1. Offer the product for sale from the initial advert. This is normally called 'off the page' advertising and means taking out a large advert.

2. Invite the public to write/phone in for free information concerning the product (two stage selling) - these are smaller adverts. For most things I prefer this method.

Now you also have five major media outlets for your advertising which are newspapers (both regional and national), magazines, the Internet, TV, and radio. As well as the media, you have the power of press releases and competitions that you can use. You also have direct mail. As a beginner I would stay of out TV and radio for the moment. I would definitely use newspapers, magazines, press releases, competitions and direct mail.

Newspapers

Although it is true that newspapers are losing some market share, there are still many larger regional and national newspapers that are worth using. Newspapers are ideal testing grounds for products, since the advertisements can be relatively cheap and your advert can appear within days of it being placed. Newspapers also offer an instant response. If one of my adverts appeared in a newspaper on a Monday, I would start receiving calls from 7 a.m. that day.

The downside with a newspaper is its short life; if the advert is in Monday's paper, it would pull in the most response on a Monday with some follow-through to Tuesday, but after that the advert will be finished because newspapers get thrown away very quickly. The other point to remember about a newspaper is that it is very general and although you can target your market by having your advert placed in a certain section i.e. the business section, your product needs to be fairly general to work in a newspaper.

How the paper is divided

Most newspapers have special days and sections, for example, Wednesday is money, Thursday is travel, etc. You may find that if your product relates to one of these days, then you should advertise on this day. For instance, if your product is a 'How to cut your tax bill' book, you could advertise on the money day, or on or around the financial pages.

There are two types of adverts: CLASSIFIED ADS and DISPLAY ADS. Classified adverts are composed of words only, in ordinary type, and listed under the heading supplied by the publication itself. Classified adverts are charged either by the word or by the line.

Display adverts are where you only buy the space that you use, i.e. 1/2 a page, 1/8 of a page, or 1/16 of a page. I mainly buy the exact space, such as a 5cm x 2 column advert. Newspapers normally sell the column by the width. The column width can vary from paper to paper and can also depend on whether the newspaper is a tabloid (i.e. The Sun) or a broadsheet (i.e. the Daily Telegraph). In a tabloid the typical column width is 3.1 cm, so my 5cm x 2 column advert would be 5cm x 6cm. In a display advert you can have pictures, diagrams, and boxes and you can use different typefaces, which allow you to produce a higher impact advert.

Reference publications

British Rate and Data (BRAD) will provide all the information you need concerning rates, printing specifications, circulations, etc. on almost all the newspapers and periodicals in the UK. BRAD is generally kept in the reference section of a public library.

Profile

When selecting a newspaper you need to know about the type of person who is going to read it. The person who reads the Financial Times will not be the same as the person who reads the Daily Mirror. The Audit Bureau of Circulation (ABC) provides information on circulation and readership.

Readers are graded into classes, according to the reader's occupation and other characteristics. For example, A = Managerial, B = Professional, C1 = Administrators, C2 = skilled/semi-skilled labourers and D = unskilled labourers.

These classes give some indication of the reader's lifestyle, level of education, attitude, and purchasing power, which are all very important factors when deciding whether the profile matches your product.

Media packs and sample copies

If you contact the advertising department of your chosen newspaper or magazine, they will send you a free sample copy of the publication and a media pack, which contains their advertising rates and profile details.

Tip: When you advertise in a publication it is very common to receive calls from sales people who work for other newspapers/magazines, wanting you to advertise in their publication. Some of them will be from publications that you may have heard of, but many will be unknown; therefore, ALWAYS ensure you get a real copy and a media pack first, before you advertise. I've had so many sales people call me, telling me that they have a special deal and I must place the advert right now! I would never do that unless I saw a real copy of the publication and a media pack. Before placing an advert in a newspaper, I would buy at least one week's worth of the newspaper if it's a daily, or a few editions if it's a monthly. Taking the example of a daily newspaper, if you look at every day's paper, you will then be able to see all the different sections/different daily features and you can then decide which day suits you best.

Magazines

Magazines are a very good type of media for mail order. While it takes longer for your advert to appear, magazines have a longer life than newspapers. People tend to keep magazines for months and even years, but never keep a newspaper for longer than a few days. Magazines are also left in doctor's/dentist's waiting rooms and offices.

The big advantage with magazines is that they are targeted. If you are looking to attract fashion-conscious women, then you can advertise in women's fashion magazines. I believe that newspaper circulations are dropping and magazine circulations are rising, because people are becoming more focused and interested in their selected interests. If you are a young woman, why should you buy a daily newspaper which has sport, financial news, motor news, etc. in it, when all you are interested in is fashion? In the UK at the time of writing this, there hasn't been a launch of a new daily national newspaper for years, whereas there seems to be a new magazine launch every week.

Your research into different magazines will give you a solid foundation and 'feel' for the types of products advertised in the various publications. Hobby or sport magazines lend themselves to mail order, since the readers are always on the lookout for an article that could assist or benefit them in some way. Trade journals provide a perfect vehicle for specialised products which appeal to only one particular segment of society, such as lawyers, architects, accountants or hoteliers.

Choosing the right magazine or newspaper

Q: If you pick up a magazine and find that there isn't a single mail order type of advert in it, do you think that this is a good sign or a bad sign?

A: It's a bad sign. Let me explain why: it is better to follow the leader than to be a pioneer. You see, if a magazine carries mail order adverts, month in month out, you can safely say that the magazine is working or the advertiser wouldn't be there. So if the advert is working for other mail order advertisers, it is likely that the magazine will work for you as well.

I have noticed that Saturday's national newspapers carry many mail order adverts (buy a copy and see for yourself), so you can safely say that Saturday must be a good day for mail order advertising. The Sunday colour magazine supplements are also very popular with mail order adverts, possibly because people are more relaxed on a Sunday and buy more.

Summary

Matching the right publication to your product is very important and you must spend some time researching the various publications carefully. Good research will avoid you making costly mistakes. For example, choosing the right section of the newspaper and choosing the right day makes a big difference. Watching other advertisers is the key. I quickly learnt that I could have the best advert position, with the best copy and a brilliant headline, but if the publication was the wrong publication for my offer, then I would get little or no response.

Exquisite words

Choose the right words to use in an advert or sales letter and you win, choose the wrong ones and you lose. Over the next few pages I will give you as much information as possible which will increase your chances of selling your products. At the back of the book I have listed some excellent books which look into advertising and marketing in further detail and I suggest you invest in a few of them.

What makes someone respond or look at an advert?

In nearly all cases it is the headline. The words at the top of the advert in large print are read first; if the reader is interested he will continue and if not, he's on to the next page. The headline is the appetiser or the hook; it should appeal to the reader in some way and provide a striking statement or promise of some benefit. I will go into this in depth in a moment as this is very important, but in a nutshell people are basically very self-centred and respond to appeals that promise gratification in some personal or intimate aspect of their life, improvement in their status, increasing their income, admiration, love and success, etc.

I have spent a great deal of time researching and looking into what people want out of a product or service and listed below are my findings. A headline either in an advert or sales letter that can appeal to one of these categories is a winner. These categories are in no particular order and they are all winners:

1. Earning money. I don't know anyone who isn't interested in this!

2. Improving health. There are very few people who can say they are 100% happy with their health.

3. Saving time - everyone wants to do this.

4. Being appreciated by others. People like to feel special and wanted. They also like to receive compliments.

5. Improving appearance and being fashionable.

6. Avoiding criticism and pain.
7. Avoiding losing money or possessions. Everybody likes to think that they are smart with money and they haven't been taken for a ride. Ask anyone who has achieved something (for example, a nice house) what their biggest fear is, and it will probably be losing their assets.
8. Leisure.
9. Improving social status and getting promoted.
10. Dating and relationships.
11. Avoiding work and/or effort.
12. Security and comfort in old age. This concern starts later on in life - no one wants to end up in a state-run nursing home.

You will no doubt be interested in some or all of these twelve categories.

Anyway, back to adverts and headlines.

"On average, five times as many people read the body copy. It follows that, unless your headline sells your product, you have wasted 90% of your money." **David Ogilvy**

Words that work in an advert

Some of the words that I will list here have been used for many years and although they may sound clichéd and they are used over and over again, it's because they work, believe me.

Words to use: NEW, AMAZING, STARTLING, REVOLUTIONARY, MIRACLE, THE TRUTH, ANNOUNCING, NOW, SUDDENLY, AT LAST, LAST CHANCE, HOW TO, WANTED, EASY, FREE, COMPARE, DISCOVER, BE A, DO YOU.

The two most effective words that you can use in an advert are FREE and NEW. Look at any successful direct mail adverts or sales letters and I guarantee you that you'll see these words used. Watch the infomercials on satellite TV and you will see and hear words like, 'AMAZING DISCOVERIES' and 'ANNOUNCING THE NEW REVOLUTIONARY...' - these people know what they are doing.

Spend time on your headline and never ever run an advert without one. In larger adverts you will tend to have a headline and a sub-headline. <u>I cannot stress enough how important the headline is.</u>

Here are a few tried and tested ways that you can start your headline:

How to...(One of my favourites)

Seven steps to...

The secret to...

Are you...

An absolutely surefire way to...

Should you...

Your guide to...

TIP: Anyone who is thinking of writing a book, manual, or marketing a video, should remember that the title is very important. I treat the title of my books and videos just like headlines and I use many of the same words. A good opening title for any book or video is 'How to'.

WARNING: Don't try to be clever in a headline; that's what advertising agencies do and they normally end up killing the response. Your headline should be direct and easy to understand.

HOW TO CUT YOUR HEATING BILLS NOW!

This is a very direct headline with short words and is not too long. I like to keep my headlines down to 10 or 15 words maximum.

An advertising agency style headline is, 'If every wife knew what every widow knows, no husband would be without life insurance.' This is a clever headline but it will not grab the reader's attention and most people will not understand it - do you understand what the story is?

Here is the key to writing a good advert, sales letter, press release or sales speech:

A = Attention. Grab the reader with a powerful headline or opening.

I = Interest. Keep them interested, make the copy persuasive yet informative and make the copy believable; back up any claims with research and testimonials.

D = Desire. Make them want to know more and make them desire your product or service; you want the reader to feel 'this is what I have always been looking for' or 'this is the answer to my dreams'.

A = Action. Ask for an action - phone now or return the coupon - and close the sale.

The first paragraph

The next step to a good advert is the first paragraph. We've got the reader past the headline but we now need to keep them reading; we need to get them excited, worried, curious, or whatever it takes.

For example: Did you know that thousands of men and women are making £500 a week plus, working from home in their spare time?

Or: It's hard to believe but it's true - you are currently wasting thousands of pounds in tax benefits because you simply don't know how to claim what is legally yours.

Body copy

This is where the main copy goes and depending on the size of your advert and the type of offer, this is where you list all the benefits and facts to the reader. The body copy needs to be easy to read, believable, and able to sell the idea to the reader. It needs to explain how your product, book, service, etc. will benefit the reader. It is pointless saying in your copy, 'My company is the best; we've been in business for years and we're the biggest...' - this is rubbish and the reader will say, 'So what!'

The reader is selfish, self–centred and is reading your advert or sales letter for his pleasure and to see what's in it for him. Remember these letters: WII FM. No, it's not a new radio station! It's 'What's in it for me?' which is the question that everyone really wants to know the answer to; people want the BENEFITS, such as:

- The stainless-steel chopping blade, which means it's easy to clean, chops quickly and easily with no effort and will stay sharp forever, saving you time and money.
- Superwax polish gives your car a long-lasting, showroom shine. Easy to apply within 20 minutes, goes on and comes off with the minimum amount of effort and leaves you more time to drive your car instead of polishing it.

See how these examples give the benefits to the customer; they tell the customer what they want to know and what the benefits are to them. If your advert is full of 'WE ARE' then scrap it and start again. You should have 'YOU WILL' and 'YOU' and also make sure that there are not too many 'I', 'We', 'My' or 'Our' words in your advert or sales letter.

A point about the length of the copy

You can never have too much copy, but you can have boring copy. I often see full-page adverts with sometimes no more than ten words in them - what a waste! It has been proven time and time again that it is the copy combined with a picture that sells, not just a picture. Long text copy can also be made to look interesting by using a good layout, using appropriate paragraphs and using bullet points (•). A quick point on using photos in adverts or sales letters: make sure that you write a small caption underneath it or beside it as some people will see a photo and not understand what it is trying to represent; the caption will also reinforce the photo's message.

In sales letters you can have longer copy, but obviously with an advert because you are paying by the centimetre, space is a premium. Don't make the mistake of trying to cram a full off-the-page advert into a small space, it normally doesn't work. If you cannot afford to go for a bigger advert, then you need to go for a two-step advert.

TIP: Editorial is read and believed far more than adverts; that is why many of my adverts are set to look like newspaper articles. A good way to tell if your copy is too cramped and hard to read is to look at it at the end of the day when your eyes are quite tired; now if you find it hard to read, then so will your potential customers.

Closing copy

This is the action space - it's amazing how many adverts don't ask for any action or don't try to close the sale. Even if you are not asking for any money or commitment at this stage, you still need to make the reader act.

For example: 'Phone now for your FREE 24-page report, which will reveal the tax secrets you should know.'

Or: 'Take action today for the special introductory offer of only £19.95. You too can be enjoying the benefits of..."

Don't be afraid to tell the reader what they should do next.

Summary on advertising

There is no way that I can tell you everything about advertising in such a short space; however, if you stick to the guidelines that I have given here, you will have a far better advert than most and you'll certainly have a better advert than any advertising agency could produce for you.

I have listed some of my favourite books on advertising at the back of this book, which are worth investing in. You can never know too much about advertising and marketing.

Chapter 8

Sales letters and direct mail

I want to start by saying, 'There is no such thing as junk mail' - if someone calls your mailing piece junk mail then you've made either one of these mistakes or possibly both:

Mistake 1

You've made your sales piece look like all the other stupid banks, insurance companies, book clubs, etc. who haven't got a clue about direct mail and take their advice from advertising agencies, who are worse than their clients - talk about the blind leading the blind!

Mistake 2

You're mailing the letter to the wrong person.

Bad direct mail

Let's deal with Mistake 1. No doubt you've received mail from life insurance companies, banks, book clubs, etc. In most cases you put them in the bin without even opening them! You know what they are trying to sell you before you even open the envelope, because they have useless teaser copy on the envelope or they have the company's name and logo on the envelope; as if that isn't bad enough, they send you the letter by MAILSORT, or BULK MAIL as they call it in the USA, which means that you and another 10 million others have received this 'special message'.

Why do these big sensible companies do it?

Well firstly, they have more money than sense and they are so big that no one normally knows what's going on; secondly, they do get some results, because if you mail 10 million letters out, even with a bad mail piece and teaser copy all over the envelope, there will always be a few fools who will respond! These companies use the 'shotgun approach' - they guess that if they fire enough bullets they are bound to hit something!

Now, I'd like to think that we are a little bit smarter than these big companies and I know a few things about successful direct mail. In the next few pages I will tell you the right way to use direct mail.

Mistake 2

Now to the second mistake, a good piece of direct mail should be addressed to someone who is interested in what the letter is selling - simple isn't it? If I receive a letter trying to get me to subscribe to Bodybuilding Weekly, I class that as JUNK MAIL. I am not interested in bodybuilding and I don't plan to take it up either! Now if I receive a sales letter about investing money or the latest computer software, then I am interested in that and as long as the mailing piece is good, it will certainly not go in the bin.

Making money with good direct mail

Direct mail works. Get it right and you will be making money so quickly, you won't know what's hit you! You'll be laughing all the way to the bank every day with huge piles of cheques and if you accept credit cards, your terminal will be doing overtime!

It's hard to describe in words the excitement and feelings that a successful direct mail project will provide; hopefully in the near future you'll experience it first-hand. At the end of this section I will show you how a winning sales letter can turn a few hundred pounds into a million pounds!

So why does my direct mail work?

Well first of all, my direct mail is targeted; I don't just write to any old fool, I qualify the person who I am writing to before I start. By using the RIGHT MAILING LIST, I have the secret information about the recipient. Now there is nothing underhand about the way I get my information; it's from the lists that are in BRAD, which I have already mentioned, and by getting more information from the list broker or list owner.

As well as good research I use recent lists and I use lists of buyers, not enquirers. I don't mind paying extra money for fresh, good-quality names and addresses - it's worth it. I also use buyers because they have parted with money before, which means that they are more qualified. Unlike the big insurance companies, I want the recipient to enjoy reading my sales letter and I want them to respond and buy from me. So the first key is to match the right person to the right offer. If I am selling a subscription to Bodybuilding Weekly, I will look through BRAD and find a list of people who are interested in Bodybuilding Fitness.

The mailing piece

In this section I will tell you how to put together a good mailing piece.

The envelope

First of all, never, ever, use teaser copy on the envelope. The envelope should not have anything on it, other than possibly a return address (no company name) and possibly PRIVATE & CONFIDENTIAL, TO BE OPENED BY ADDRESSEE ONLY or URGENT FIRST CLASS MAIL.

TIP: If you are using two-step advertising and you're sending out information to an enquirer, it is a good idea to make up a stamp that says, 'Here is the important information that you have requested' - it will normally get your letter read before everyone else's.

And that's it. The name and address can either be handwritten if it's a small mailing, directly printed onto the envelope, or you can use a window envelope. Stick to a white envelope for most mailings. It all depends on the volume of mail that you are sending out. I've used hand-addressed envelopes, directly printed envelopes, and window envelopes, and all three methods have worked fine. I would never use STICKY LABELS on a piece of mail as it looks like JUNK MAIL.

Now I have read books which say that you should print on your envelope because it is your 'shop front'. Maybe 20 years ago printing on an envelope may have worked, but today people are smarter; they probably get lots of direct mail and they are time-starved.

Stamps

A real postage stamp with a postmark on it is the best option to make your letter look personal. If you are a real perfectionist you can use a colourful stamp that has some sort of appeal to your reader, such as sports or flowers.

A few direct mail companies have also started to mail out from abroad, so that the envelope has a foreign stamp and postmark on it. I know a timeshare company who did this very successfully.

Let's summarise the envelope before we go any further. If you can't get the recipient to even open your letter, then everything else is pointless. See how I am making the envelope a mystery; you can't tell anything from the envelope: no company name, logo, or teaser copy. There is no way that anyone throws mail away when they don't know what's inside it - it could be money for all they know. I always use a thicker envelope so that you can't tell what's inside the envelope by holding it up.

The letter

Using the discreet envelope method, you will get past the bin. But you're not home and dry yet, far from it; you now need to get the recipient to read your letter. The basics here are the same as a newspaper or magazine advert: we need a headline, hook, statement, etc. that will appeal to the reader. Imagine that the reader is the judge and jury; before I set the stage, this is a unique concept and way of thinking and if any other book tells you this, then they copied it from me!

Anyway, imagine that you have been wrongly accused of a crime and you are defending yourself; your sales letter is your defence and the customer is the JUDGE and JURY. If you convince him/her, then you've got their order. If you don't convince them, then your sales letter goes to jail (well in the bin, but it's the same thing really!)

So what do we need to defend ourselves? We need to make a very strong argument, we need to appeal to the judge, we need to make our story believable, we need to back up our claims and finally, we need to pull a few rabbits out of a hat as a finale and close our case.

Wow! Sounds dramatic, but writing winning sales letters is dramatic - it's the difference between eating bread and water for dinner or freshly squeezed juice and lobster!

Back to sales letters...

Now remember that we have targeted this person so we should know a little bit about them as we know what they've purchased in the past. A great example of headline writing was a letter sent to recent investors of certain companies. The letter was selling investment books and an investment newsletter. The headline was: **Your shares in British Telecom - should you buy more, sell, or hold them?**

Now imagine receiving this letter and you are a shareholder in British Telecom - would you read it? Of course you would. Now for those of you saying, 'How did they know he had shares in British Telecom?' it's simple: you can buy shareholders' names and addresses. If you look in BRAD you'll see millions of them.

Another great headline was: **Those valuable coins you've recently bought, are they real?**

Again, we know that the reader has just bought valuable coins, because his name is on a list of valuable coin collectors. This headline was used for a product called the 'Gold Tester'. It's a sort of electronic pen and when you run it over metal, a light indicates whether it is gold, how pure the gold is, or if isn't gold at all (fake).

The sub-headline

This is where you can expand a bit on the headline, for instance, a sub-headline for the gold tester offer could be: **"Introducing a new and amazing way to test gold coins within seconds."**

TIP: It seems that people remember and believe headlines that are in quotations marks, for example, "Discover how to prevent cancer".

The salutation

The best salutation and one that I nearly always use is the person's name, i.e. Dear Mr Smith, or Dear Mrs Davidson. It takes some time and effort to get your computer to mail-merge the address, but it's worth it. It makes the letter look personal and official. If you can't manage mail-merge then you could get a bureau to do it for you.

PLEASE DO NOT USE Dear Friend, especially in the UK. I suggest that if you can't use a personal salutation, you should skip it altogether and just go straight into your letter.

Opening paragraph

This is the same as newspaper or magazine advertising - we've got the reader past the headline but we need to keep them reading and we need to get them excited, worried, curious, or whatever.

The body copy

This is the main part of the letter which needs to tell all. Remember what I said earlier about WII FM (What's in it for me?)- keep answering that regularly during the letter. Also, keep the letter personal, as if it's to someone you already know. A technique that I use in letter writing is to ask questions and answer them myself. I try to answer any questions that I think the reader would ask, as if I were talking face to face with them, for example:

Can you really make money from the goldfish business?

Yes, there are thousands of men and women all over the country who are earning excellent first and second incomes from goldfish breeding.

A good layout, font, bullets, bold test, underlining and italics

It is important to make the letter easy to read and you need to leave some white space or the eye will drown in a sea of words. Don't let the sentence go from edge to edge; leave a margin at both ends because the reader's eye can only go so far across the page. Make sure the space between each word is enough and the space between each line is adequate. These parameters can easily be changed on your Microsoft Word or desktop publisher so you can experiment with different settings. Make sure that you keep your paragraphs fairly short and use bullet points to make the benefits stand out, such as:

- Learn how to get FREE advertising!
- Discover the secrets that advertising agencies won't tell you!
- Why starting on a limited budget is an advantage!

I also use a sub-headline to break up any large blocks of text, which I normally centre, for example, 'Free bonus report', 'Why you must take action today', or 'Full Money Back Guarantee if you are not 100% satisfied'.

Fonts

The only two fonts that I use for the body copy are Arial, which looks like this: AaBbCcDdEeFf and gives a typewriter look, and Bookman, which is the font this book has been written in and is fairly easy to read. For big headlines I like **Switzerland Black.**

A good graphic designer will tell you never to use more than two fonts in an advert and I think that is very good advice for a sales letter.

Bold text, underlining and italics

These features should be used in a good sales letter but you must not overdo it. Treat them as if they are special effects and less is more. If you underline every other line it will look terrible and I once saw a company's sales letter who did this in red!

Bold text is good for sub-headlines and the occasional line. Italics can be very hard to read and I don't often use them.

Back to the sales letter...

Testimonials, quotes, and research

These are all good ways to break up your sales letter and most importantly, they add credibility and back up your claims. Sales letters need to be believable and backing up your claims reinforces your message.

NOTE: I want to tell you about making your offer sound too good; unfortunately, many people are negatively programmed and if your offer sounds too far-fetched, even though it's true, you can lose a lot of sales.

Let me give you an example: Someone I knew ran the headline, 'Earn £25,000 a year running your own successful part-time publishing business'. Now I knew that this was a realistic figure and in fact many people would make far more than that, yet when he changed the headline to 'Earn £1,000 a month running your own successful part-time publishing business', he had a far better response. It seems that people BELIEVED that they could make an extra £1,000 a month, but they didn't believe they could make £25,000 a year! So remember this story - sometimes you have to actually scale down the offer.

Testimonials

Hopefully you will receive letters from satisfied customers and I suggest that you write back to them, thanking them for their kind remarks and requesting permission from them to use extracts of their letter in your marketing material.

Another way to obtain feedback and comments which can be used is to mail out a questionnaire to people who have recently purchased your product. Ask them a simple question and ask them for a brief comment on what they liked about XYZ. On the questionnaire you need to state that some quotes may be used by the company in their promotional material, however, assure the customer that you will not give out their address and that their confidentiality will be respected. Also state that you reserve the right to edit their testimonial. You MUST always give the customer something back if you expect them to help you. I would suggest a headline on your letter along the lines of, 'Help us with our marketing and you can claim a FREE gift.' The gift could be a pen, book, report, video, or a discount voucher off future orders. By the way, if anyone wants to write to me with some nice, honest comments about this book then please do. There's a form at the back of this book and YES, you will get a FREE gift for your time and effort. You can never have enough feedback.

You wouldn't normally print the whole testimonial letter; you would just choose few lines. Here are few testimonial letters:

- “I really enjoy reading your marketing newsletter. It is the best resource available. Keep up the good work” – J.Y. Hampton, VA.
- “Here’s my cheque for the renewal of my subscription to the Video Marketing Letter. I value your tips highly.” – D.S. Hope, London.
- “Superb! Literally hundreds of ideas which will make or save me more than ten times the cost of the seminar!” G. Thomas, Atlanta, GA.

Quotes and research

Statements such as ‘Dr Brown, a professor at the London University, recently tested XYZ and his tests concluded that the XYZ was one of the best ways to increase your longevity.’

Or: ‘A recent article in the Wall Street Journal claimed that over 54% of people are terrified of speaking in public.’

Obviously research and quotes have to be true and do need to originate from the source you say that they do.

Free gifts, bonuses, and discounts prompt action

People like to get something for nothing. Remember in my exquisite words, FREE was one of the best words. Offering an extra bonus, such as a videotape or report, can clinch the deal. If you remember the investment newsletter that we mentioned earlier, with the headline 'Your shares in British Telecom - should you buy more, sell, or hold them?' Well the free bonus with that was a special report on British Telecom shares, which was a very powerful premium, and I'm sure that many people bought the newsletter just to get the report!

The aim of the premium (bonus) is to give something that the reader thinks is very expensive, yet costs you very little.

A discount or extra premium for prompt action

The aim of our sales letter is to make the reader act immediately; we need to create some urgency and we want the reader's order now, not in 12 months' time. Therefore, we need to politely ask the reader to send his money now. It's amazing how many companies don't offer any incentives to the reader to act immediately. I use words to the effect of: Act today and you will qualify for an extra free gift. Or: If you act promptly and submit your order to us before 1st August XXXX, we will also include an extra bonus as a special thank you for acting promptly.

Price

A lot of people ask me when they should spill the beans and reveal the price. In most cases leave it until the end - by then you will have stated your case to the reader, who really is the JUDGE, and they will have read everything you've had to say and if you've made your case strong enough, the price will be insignificant. I have occasionally used the price in the headline, for example, 'Now for only £5 a week you can own...'

P.S.

A few people have asked me if I use a P.S. because I have forgotten something - I don't think so! The P.S. that I use and many other successful direct mailers use is very deliberate; in fact, now I never send any newsletters without a P.S. and in many cases I have a P.P.S.

I don't know why, but people always take note of a P.S. and that's all you should know. Use a P.S. to summarise your offer and state the strongest benefits - a P.S. is really like a headline, but at the end of the letter.

For example: **P.S.** Don't forget that if you order today you will receive the full 'How to breed goldfish course', the free XYZ, and the special bonus XYZ, not for the normal price of £50.00 but for the special price of only £17.77.

Or: **P.S.** Act today because you really can't afford to waste another day without the XYZ. Don't forget with our FULL MONEY BACK GUARANTEE, you have nothing to lose and everything to gain.

Signature

Never send a letter without a signature. I have signed up to 5,000 mailings by hand; it is a pain but it's worth it. Use blue ink and (if you can) use an ink pen to give a thicker look to your signature; this is very impressive and gives the ultimate personal look.

For larger mailings your printer will have to print your signature and although it won't look as good as the real thing, as long as they use a good blue ink, the match will be acceptable. You can now get your signature made into a rubber stamp.

Brochures

For many products and services a good sales letter alone will not be enough and you will need a sales brochure. Before I go any further, never mail out just a sales brochure on its own - without a letter it doesn't work. I've found the best combination is a good sales letter and a fairly brief brochure. A brochure should be designed to look interesting and be informative, but at the same time, you must remember that its purpose is to sell the product or service. A good brochure should be a joy to read, look good and ultimately help to finish your sale. Remember to think of the customer first in the brochure: list all the benefits to the reader and keep technical terms down to a minimum. If you must have a technical specification page then put it at the back somewhere. A good brochure should be well planned and needs to hold the reader's attention. Start the brochure with an introduction, then go on to the main benefits and then close the brochure with a strong summary.

Tip: It's a good idea to have a quote or an important statement towards the bottom of the page, such as: "I've never used an easier car polish," - Bill Green, Texas; or 'A lifetime guarantee comes as standard when you buy an ABC.' Another tip is to have a phone number and fax number at the bottom of each page.

The order form

The order form tends to be the most underrated part of the direct mail package, yet it is crucial to your success - if no one fills in the order form then you are finished!

Whenever I design an order form I try to make it as easy as possible for the customer to complete. I leave lots of space and I try to use tick boxes rather than make the client have to write something. If an order form is difficult to fill in, then the prospective client may give up or put the form to one side.

On many of my mailings I already fill in as much as I can on the order form, such as their name, address, and account number. I would then add 'If the details shown here are incorrect, then please amend accordingly.' (See sample order form)

The other thing I always do is to summarise the offer again on the order form. I also try to make the client feel good about making the order, for example:

Yes, I am ready to make money with the ABC course. Please rush me the course at the special reduced introductory price of £29.77. I understand that if I am not 100% satisfied with the course I can return it for a refund. Please also send me my FREE BONUS. I enclose my cheque, postal order, draft, made payable to 'ABC' for £29.77. Alternatively, please debit my credit card as below.

You should also state the expiry date of the offer, which can be stamped on the order form, for example: This order must be received at our office no later than Friday 26th December 2015.

A catalogue-type order form

If you are selling more than one product then you will not know the total price, but you can still state your offer and your guarantee. On an order form I always like the first item to be listed as FREE. For example, say the free gift is a Rolex watch, the order form would look like this: 1 Gold Rolex Watch = FREE

Sample order form/coupon

This form is the type used when you have a fixed price and product.

NO RISK TRIAL

Mr. A.N Other

123 Anytown

Sample

AB1 1AB

If details shown are incorrect then please amend accordingly.

Ref: 1345678

YES, I am ready to make money with the ABC course. Please rush me the course at the special reduced introductory price of £29.77. I understand that if I am not 100% satisfied with the course I can return it for a refund. Please also send me my FREE BONUS as I am ordering before the 26th December 2015.

I enclose my cheque/postal order/draft made payable to "ABC" for £29.77, alternatively please debit my credit card as below'

Visa ☐ Mastercard ☐ Amex ☐ Delta ☐ Switch

☐

Credit/debit card expiry date: ☐☐☐☐☐

SWITCH ONLY (please state issue number) ☐

Once completed please return in the prepaid envelope enclosed.

ABC, 123 Post Road, Anytown, AB2 1AB.

If paying by credit/debit card you can fax your order to: 1234 5678

We thank you for your order and your course will be rushed to you by return.

Sample order form/coupon

This form is the type to use when you have more than one product, such as with a catalogue, where you do not know what the total order will be.

The Mother of ALL OFFERS?????

We put together a package of everything you'll need to get your video production business off the ground. We call it the 'Mother of all Offers' because it includes everything but the kitchen sink.....
This is what you get:

- ☐ Desktop Video for profit video tape – (see description on page 3)
- ☐ Desktop Video & the Amiga video tape – (see description on page 4)
- ☐ Setting up a Low Budget Video Studio video tape – (see description page 4)
- ☐ Advanced Guide to Guerrilla Video tape
- ☐ Three years of The Video Marketing Letter Back Issues (over 300 pages on how to make money as an independent video producer)
- ☐ Plus, a one year subscription to The Video Marketing Letter.

This is over $400 worth of goodies, but in our "Mother" offer, you get it all for $189!!! And it doesn't stop there either. With the "Mother" offer you also get Free use of our Video Technical Hotline, and opportunities to discuss your video needs with our studio professionals. What a deal!

#GM119 THE MOTHER of ALL OFFERS... $189

ORDER FORM

Name:____
Street:____

City:____
State: __________________ Zip: __________________

Daytime Phone # : ________________________________

Item #	QTY	Item Description	Price	Total
GM800	1	Guerilla Video Hour	FREE	
My cheques or MO is enclosed for $ Make cheques payable to Group M (COO Orders must be placed by phone)			Subtotal	
			S & H	$4.00
			Total	

Card No.

☐☐☐☐☐☐☐☐☐☐☐☐☐☐☐☐

Exp Date: ☐☐☐☐☐
Please sign:____
Tel : 1 800 237 5188
Group M Productions 321 Quachita Ave. Hot Springs, AR 71901

TIP: More and more people have access to fax machines these days, so make sure that you encourage orders to be faxed to you if payment is made by debit/credit cards.

Thank the customer

Make sure you have something like 'Thank you for your order', or 'We appreciate your business and we will dispatch your order as soon as possible.' Customers like to think that they are smart and they are doing the right thing by dealing with you and thanking them is a good way to reassure them.

How to judge if your order form is any good

Once you have produced your order form, print one out and take a good look at it and imagine that you are the customer - does it look easy to fill in and does it inspire confidence? Another way is to test the form yourself. Give yourself a maximum of two minutes to fill in the order form - if you find it difficult, then the chances are that your customers will as well.

Money back guarantee

To be taken seriously in direct mail today, you must offer a money back guarantee. You could hold back the postage and packaging charge but most companies give a full money back guarantee. Most people work on a 30 day money back guarantee, whereas some companies offer up to 12 months - it all depends on your product.

A money back guarantee inspires confidence in your company and helps to take the risk out of buying. As long as your product is good and you ship it correctly and on time, you shouldn't get more than 1-2% back, which you can live with. In most cases you can sell the returns on again.

Note: Take care when packaging your goods: use padded envelopes, packing material, etc. and although it costs a bit extra and takes a little time, it's worth it. There is nothing worse than customers screaming on the phone that the goods have arrived in a damaged state. If you are shipping goods overseas, then make sure that you pack with even more care.

Prepaid envelopes

Never expect a customer to find an envelope and a stamp and then write your address out - it's too hard. Always enclose a reply paid envelope, which is printed with your address on it and no stamp is required. The extra cost is worth it.

Note: Occasionally a prepaid envelope may be missed out or lost by the potential client, so make sure that you have your address printed on the order form as a backup.

Frequently Answered Question (FAQ) sheet

This is probably one of the best things that you can add to a direct mail package. In my various direct mail businesses I would listen to what people were asking and from these questions, together with other questions I imagined the customers would want to know the answers to, I would produce a question and answer sheet. For example:

Q. Can I work from home?

A. Yes, many people started or still work from home.

Q. What happens if I need help?

A. Once you join you will be given a special telephone number which is manned from 8.30 a.m. – 6.30 p.m. weekdays and 8.30 a.m. – 1 p.m. Saturdays. We will answer your questions immediately or come back to you within a few minutes.

Many of the questions would have already been previously answered in your brochure; however, stating them again in this format helps.

Note: The aim of your sales letter and brochure is to sell to the customer from start to finish. Successful mail order entrepreneurs have sold to millions of people without them ever calling their offices and that is your aim. The last thing you want is millions of people on the phone with long lists of questions; if you're getting that then your brochure/sales letter is letting you down.

Selling Words

Here I will explain some extra techniques which can be used to increase your hit rate and your profits.

Attach a post-it note to the letter

Now if you're mailing out thousands of letters you will not want to hand write each note, but there are now companies that will print on a post-it note for you. I would suggest that you hand write the note and then get it printed in a good blue ink, so that it looks handwritten.

What to say on the note:

'Take action today, you won't regret it!'

'You will be delighted with the results from XYZ, I guarantee it!'

'This is the best offer that I have ever made; don't let it pass you by!'

Use a lift letter

This is where you include a short letter in addition to your primary letter in a direct mailing. The aim of the lift letter is to give a second opinion or a different opinion. It should be written in a different style to the main letter and preferably signed or endorsed by someone else, other than the main letter writer.

The lift letter should have a handwritten look to it or look as if it's been written on an old typewriter. The letter should also be put in a separate small envelope with words printed on the front such as:

'Looking for another professional's opinion?'

'Still not convinced? Then open this envelope!'

'Are you sceptical? Open this envelope for more proof!'

The letter should go along the lines of a testimonial or endorsement, such as:

'I've been using XYZ for ten years now and I can remember being wary about the claims that were made, but I can truly say that it has been the best...'

How to make the customer buy more than they planned

This technique is ideal if you are mailing out a catalogue of products which are all related. Let's say that we are mailing out a catalogue of 'how to videos' - the prospective client has gone through the catalogue and maybe seen a few videos that he likes and one or two others that he definitely likes;

now right at the end, try a 'Mother of all offers' - this is where you state that the client can have one of everything in the catalogue for a special price. Believe me, even if you have to cut your margins a little, it's worth having an offer like this.

Buy 2 get 1 free

This is very successful in retail stores at the moment and can work very well in mail order as well. Another good idea is to have on your order form something like 'Buy a second XYZ for a friend or a member of your family for only £???' and offer them a good price.

Response rates and testing

Let's talk about the bottom line, which is money. If you follow everything I have told you up till now, you will have a winning sales letter and as long as you are mailing out to a good list, then you are going to make money. Now it's impossible for me to tell you how much - you will only find this out once you have sent out an initial test mailing, which should be around 2,000 pieces. Now many people like to talk about what percentage response they get, i.e. 1%, 3% or 10%; I never really look at percentages, all I care about is the CASH.

It's the cash that counts - response rates are for vanity, cash is for sanity!

I've had projects that have only brought in a 0.5% response, yet they made thousands of pounds because the profit margin was very high. My minimum aim is to double my money in direct mail and in almost all my projects I have done this, if not more. For example: Let's say that I am mailing out 1,000 letters and the cost to print, stamps, etc. is £400. I am selling a product for £60 which makes me £40 clear profit each time; all I need is a 2.5% response and I've brought in over £800, which is double my investment. I don't count the 0.5% as this covers the costs and shipping the product.

Costing out a project

I use a Microsoft Excel spreadsheet for costing out my direct mail; this way I can see within minutes if a project is viable, what my break-even point is and so on. The printout shows what to include in your costs: basically your printing, stamps and envelopes, etc.

Notice how hard it is to make money by selling products at £20, yet when you make £60 or £100 per sale, your break-even point is much lower.

Sample Direct Mail Marketing Evaluation	
Creative Costs	**£**
Copywriting Fee	0.00
Other Creative Costs	0.00
Total Creative Cost	**0.00**
Variable Costs	
Names (per 1,000)	85.00
Postage (per 1,000)	198.00
Printing (per 1,000)	152.00
Envelopes (per 1,000)	24.00
Labour (per 1,000)	0.00
Other Costs	0.00
Total Variable Costs	**459.00**
Fulfillment Costs	
Product Cost	15.00
Packaging Cost	1.00
Shipping Cost	4.00
Order Taking Costs	0.00
Cost of Premium	0.55
Other Fulfillment Costs	0.00
Total Fulfillment Costs	**20.55**
Product Price	**89.95**
Note: Test several product prices to determine optimum profit	
Performance Analysis	
Cost per piece to mail	0.45
Total number of letter mailed	1,000
Sales needed to break-even	6.62 0.66%
Profit on 3% response	1, 622.36
Profit on 5% response	3,010.36
Notes:	
a) Ideally, it is better to test a minimum of 3,000 names.	
b) The selection of the right mailing list is crucial for a valid test result.	
c) Notice the low break-even figure – this is what you should always be aiming for.	
You can cost out your direct mail projects with pen and paper but it's much easier to use a Microsoft Excel Spreadsheet.	

How using a sales letter and a winning direct mail offer can turn a few hundred pounds into over a million!

First of all, the technique that I will explain here has nothing to do with multilevel marketing, chain letters, or any other scams. The method I will disclose to you is totally legal and is just simple mathematics. This is the first time that I have put this in writing, but I, and many others, have done it in reality. I was reluctant to give out this secret in this book but in the end I thought, why not? I always try to give people much more value than what they paid for or expected.

So here we go: using the techniques that we have discussed in this section we can safely say that you can produce a good sales letter and offer, which brings in £100 profit for every £250 you invest; remember that many products will bring in far more, but let's stay with this figure as it makes the maths simple. Watch how by investing the profit what happens:

Table assuming only a 40% profit

Time	Starting Capital £	Net Profit £
1st Time	250	100 (+350)
2nd	350	140 (+490)
3rd	490	196 (+686)
4th	686	274 (+960)
5th	960	384 (+ 1,344)
6th	1,344	538 (+1,882)
7th	1,882	753 (+ 2,635)

8th	2,635	1,054 (+ 3,689)
9th	3,689	1,476 (+ 5,165)
10th	5,165	2,066 (+ 7,231)
11th	7,231	2,892 (+ 10,123)
12th	10,123	4,049 (+ 14,172)
13th	14, 172	5,669 (+ 19,841)
14th	19,841	7,936 (+ 27,777)
15th	27,777	11,111 (+ 38,888)
16th	38,888	15,555 (+ 54,443)
17th	54,443	21,777 (+ 76,220)
18th	76,220	30,488 (+ 106,708)
19th	106,708	42,683 (+ 149,391)
20th	149,391	59,756 (+ 209,147)
21st	209,147	83,6659 (+ 292,806)
22nd	292,806	117,122 (+ 409, 928)
23rd	409,928	163,971 (+573,899)
24th	573,899	229, 560 (+ 803, 459)
25th	803, 459	321,384 (+ 1,124,843)

And that's how simple it is; the power of direct mail can turn small profit margins into big results. Now let's answer some possible questions that you may have about this multiplying system: Firstly I've used a small starting figure of £250; if you start with £500 then of course you will achieve one million much quicker.

Secondly, I've been realistic and I have used a figure of one million; this is because if you carried on forever there will come a time when your mailings are so large that you would be mailing the whole world! What I suggest you do if you need to earn more is to find another product that makes the same return and start again.

Thirdly, in the real world the mathematics will not be as precise as the table, but the end results will be the same or very similar, so on one mailing you'll get a bit more and on another you'll get less.

This technique also works very well in the stock market and trading. Buy one company, sell it, plough profits into another, and so on.

How the same principles work in advertising

On a recent trip to America I saw someone who claims that he went from nothing to a millionaire by using the same concept of multiplying, but he did it with classified adverts.

His system was to book a small advert, selling products that would net him around US$40 from one advert, which is very realistic. He would then repeat the same advert in over 200 newspapers throughout the USA, working on US$40 x 200 - that's US$8,000 a week. He would run two or three different adverts selling different products, normally information type products. You can now see how lots of small adverts, which don't make that much money on their own, can make a big profit when added together.

Why you should go back for a 2nd, 3rd or even 4th try

Let's say that you've sent out a mailing of 1,000 letters and 50 people buy, which is a very realistic figure of 5% response. Now it makes sense to re-mail the 950 people that didn't buy, as the chances are that a second letter will normally result in at least another 25 to 30 buyers out of the 950.

You see, even with the best letter you will have people that are undecided or need a reminder to make them act. I also found that a follow-up letter was essential because some potential customers would say that they had never received the first letter.

How to re-mail

1st Reminder

The best thing is to use the same letter as the first letter and add on 'SECOND NOTICE' or 'URGENT REMINDER' - you could also print 'COPY' on the letter in the background. You should also send a new covering letter; I would start with 'Perhaps you misplaced my last letter as I have not heard from you, therefore I am enclosing another copy.'

2nd Reminder

Depending on your product you could go straight to this stage, which is the 'Last Chance/Reduced Offer' letter. Here you should explain that you have not heard from them and you would like to give them a last chance to order and as an incentive, you reduce the price slightly or you could offer them an extra special bonus. If you are selling an expensive item, you could allow the potential customer to spread the payment over two or three instalments.

A note on re-mailing rented lists

If you have rented a list of, say, business opportunity seekers, the chances are that they were for one use only; therefore, you must go back to the list broker/owner and negotiate a deal with them to re-mail the names. Most lists can be rented out at normally half the price you paid for the first time mailing. Of course, if it's your own list, i.e. people that have phoned you in reply to your advert or names that you have compiled, then of course you can re-mail them as many times as you like.

How many times should you re-mail

The simple answer to this is until it is no longer profitable. Some companies mail out four or five times and can still make it pay.

Getting ideas from other direct mail users

I suggest that you start keeping every single piece of direct mail that you receive and try to get on as many mailing lists as you can; I would also suggest that you ask your friends and family to keep unwanted direct mail and pass it on to you. It is always good to see how other companies put together a direct mail piece; look at what you think they have done wrong and make sure that you're not doing the same. You can also pick up on any good points and incorporate them into your sales letter. Try to get on the mailing lists of registered charities, Reader's Digest, Linguaphone language courses, companies selling magazine/newsletter subscriptions and any other company that is an effective user of direct mail. Take notice of how they write to you on the first, second, and third time.

Summary

Everyone reading this should use direct mail in some shape or form. Even if you are not selling a direct product, you should still use direct mail. For example, if you are an advertising agency, recruitment agency, fashion consultant, etc. then direct mail should be used to get appointments and build up your relationship with new clients. If done correctly, as previously outlined, then it will be a very cost-effective way for you to sell your product or service.

NOTE: Don't mistake direct mail with leaflets or door-to-door distribution; I've found that leaflets are not a particularly cost-effective form of marketing and they are too much like 'shotgun' marketing for my liking.

Testing is the key

I've already mentioned that you need to test your mailing piece first, normally with around 2,000 people. Testing allows you to get a feel for the offer; you will find out what people are phoning you to ask, why they are buying, what they don't like, etc. It is through testing that you can develop things like the frequently asked question sheet previously mentioned. If your mailing piece works on 2,000 then you can start mailing out to larger numbers.

What you need to know about the Post Office

If you are going to be in the direct mail/mail order business then the Post Office is going to be an important part of your business; even if you are using a private courier to ship your goods, you will still be using the Post Office to send out your mailings and responses to enquiries.

The first thing to remember is that the Post Office needs people like us - it's the businesses that keep them going, not grannies buying second class stamps! I suggest you make contact with your local sales manager and tell them that you're going into the mail order business and you would like to build up a good business relationship.

The Post Office can help you in the following ways:

1. Freepost and Business Reply. Royal Mail has a free pack on this, which will answer all your questions.

2. Postal collections. If you are mailing out 2,000 letters you don't want to have to take them to the post office, let the post office come to you! The Post Office will send a van round to pick up your mail (this is a free service if you are mailing large amounts); you can either have a daily collection or you can have a collection as and when you call them.

3. Special promotions. The Post Office wants you to succeed and have special promotions from time to time. A while back there was a promotion where you could mail 1,000 letters for the price of 800.

4. Packet Post and other special pricing arrangements. If you are a big mailer of letters or small packets over 60 grams, you could apply for Packet Post; this is where you pay per gram and not by price bands as consumers do.

As your company grows your needs will change and different Post Office services will apply.

Using a courier

Depending on the weight of your product, you will probably want to use a reliable national and international courier. A good courier is an extension to your business and gives a great image. Imagine your parcel being delivered in a shiny van by a uniformed courier - it gives a great impression to your customer.

It is also important to use a reliable courier who will deliver your goods in good condition and on time. Remember, if you make a promise of 48hrs delivery and the parcel doesn't arrive, it's YOU the customer screams at, not the courier.

When should you post your direct mail out?

I have always tried to aim for my direct mail to arrive on the potential customer's doorstep on Saturday. This means mailing out late on Thursday or Friday for First Class mail and Wednesday for Second Class.

For mailings that are mainly business addresses, aim for the mail to arrive midweek, as most businesses are not there on a Saturday and that means your mail will be opened on a Monday, which is a busy day.

For households, mail that arrives on Saturday stands more of a chance of being read, as most people still have Saturdays off and they have more time to relax and read their post. If your sales letter arrives on Monday morning, the chances are that the potential customer is harassed and the mail could end up in the bin or put to one side.

Note: If someone has requested your information from an advert, then send the information out and reply as soon as possible, regardless of the day; it is very impressive when you phone up for information and it's on your doorstep the next morning.

How to address your letter properly

If you are advertising and people are phoning in or writing in for information, it can sometimes be hard to take down the right address; however, there is a computer program which can really help with this called Quick Address. This program has all of the addresses in the UK stored in it and all you do is simply type in the postcode. For example, Jackie Smith phones up for some information; you type in her name and the next thing you ask for is her postcode; you then type this in and up pops the full address and all you need is the house number or house name.

You've no doubt experienced this when dealing with large organisations and until recently this type of software was very expensive; however, now you can get this facility from as little as £99. If you would like a free demo disk and further details, contact QAS System Ltd on 0207 498 7777 or write to them at QAS Systems Ltd, 7 Old Town, London SW4 0JT.

Chapter 9

Press releases

Press releases are a very effective form of marketing which most businesses totally ignore. Writing a good press release/article and sending it to the right people is usually the quickest and least expensive way for any business to generate a lot of new customers and orders, yet the majority of businesses do not write or make a single press release available to newspaper or magazine editors. What many people don't realise is that many magazines and newsletters depend on press releases to fill their pages.

What is a press release?

A press release is an announcement or a story that you write about your company, or a product that you believe is newsworthy. Your aim is to get the editor to either print the press release word for word, which does happen in many cases, or for the editor to write a piece based on your press release. The key is to provide something informative for the reader and at the same time plug your product and give out a contact number and/or address.

Another way to get free publicity is to write an article about a subject which you know about and that there is an interest in. The topic should be related to the product you are selling; for instance, I have written articles relating to topics in this book and at the end of the article I would plug myself, for example: Y.E. Shofola is the author of *How to occupy till Jesus comes – Wealth Creation*; to find out more about her book, telephone... or write to...

TIP: When you write a press release it should be written as though a journalist has written it from their perspective. For example, you would not say, 'I am the Director of ABC Computers and I would like to announce that I have invented a new laser printer', you would say 'Jackie Smith, the Director of ABC Computers, has invented a new laser printer.'

If you need help writing a press release you could consult a PR consultant/agency, or you could contact a journalist from a local newspaper who could write the press release for you. Most journalists are underpaid and are always looking for some freelance work.

A good format for a press release should answer:

Who – Jackie Smith/ ABC Plc/the B&B Partnership

Where – London/New York/Beijing

What – New car/computer/travel service

Why – To help small businesses/to save energy

When – Now/open on 1st January 2015

How – Details on how to get more information/the stores selling the product

A guide to getting a press release/article printed

1. Identify magazines, newsletters and newspapers whose readers are specifically interested in your product or service. You can look through BRAD for the names and addresses of magazines and newspapers.
2. Once you've identified a particular magazine or newsletter that reaches your audience, call and get a sample copy of the publication.
3. Write your press release/article in a similar style to the articles that are currently running. For instance, you could copy their typesetting style, the size of their headlines and columns, etc.
4. Proofread your press release.

5. Print the press release out on your laser printer and attach a high-quality black and white photo of your product, if applicable. Write a short covering letter and send it to the editor of the publication.

Tips:

1. Whenever you send a press release always call the magazine first; identify, and get the proper spelling of, the name of the person the press release/article should be sent to.
2. If you are promoting a product, i.e. a book or video, then tell the editor that 'A review copy is available.'
3. Send the press release in a good envelope and do not fold the press release; you could also use some cardboard to keep it from being bent.
4. Many editors will give you a call before printing your press release to ask you a few questions, so be ready to answer them in a polite and efficient manner (have a copy of the press release handy). You'll see a few samples of press releases which will give you an idea of what they look like. One is a traditional press release and one is a typeset article.

Summary

Everyone can use a press release, whether it's a new product, a book, or whether you are a consultant providing a service, you can plug yourself for FREE by using a press release.

NOTE: I've concentrated on newspapers here, but press releases can also be sent to radio or TV stations and Internet sites. Many authors have their books featured on the radio and TV, and many radio stations will ask you to go in for a live on air chat about your product or book. This is great FREE advertising.

Whatever service or product you are offering, I urge you to use press releases. I've listed a good book on the subject called *Be your own PR Man* in the reference section and I suggest you either buy a copy or take this book out from the library. This book also has excellent tips on public speaking, holding a press conference, and dealing with radio and television interviews.

Traditional press release

Sample News Release

New book information

FOR IMMEDIATE RELEASE CONTACT: Sandi Tutja 813 596 4966

PUBLISH YOUR OWN BOOK AND MAKE A FORTUNE

Bestselling author reveals insider secrets and shorts to self-publishing success

For many would be authors, the most difficult part of getting published is not the actual writing of a book. It's finding an agent or publisher who will do the work justice and recompense the author fairly. According to prolific author and seasoned self-publisher Ted Nicholas, 'The conventional publishing route is simply not open to the majority of writers, especially new ones. It is becoming more and more difficult to even get an editor interested enough to look at your manuscript, much less see the day when it rolls off the presses.

Nicholas knows a better road to publishing fame and fortune, revealed in his new guide, **HOW TO PUBLISH A BOOK & SELL A MILLION COPIES** (Enterprise *Dearborn, $19.95).

The surprising truth is that authors can benefit more from self-publishing. Once they learn the ropes, they can put in the time and hard work to promote their product that publishing companies just aren't prepared to devote to an unknown author. Even better, once their work starts selling, authors can look forward to reaping all the profits.

Those ready to cash in on their labour of love need only consult Nicholas's book. Filled with the kind of inside information and tips that can make the difference between a best seller and a flop. HOW TO PUBLISH A BOOK & SELL A MILLION COPIES gives the readers the tools and techniques to:

- Earn $1,000 a day from their publishing activities
- Develop their work - be it a book, newsletter, special report, video, audio tape or software
- Get it printed or produces a the best price
- Get free publicity
- Market and direct mail their product

An extensive appendix of resources and contacts the author has personally cultivates through the years will help readers get the additional assistance they need – worth the price of the book alone!

Nicholas himself launched Enterprise Publishing Company in 1972 with his first self-published title, HOW TO FORM YOUR OWN CORPORATION WITHOUT A LAWYER FOR UNDER $75. That book has since sold nearly one million copies, and Nicholas has been approached by just about every major publisher to its rights.

Nicholas obviously knows what works and how to sell it and HOW TO PUBLISH A BOOK & SELL A MILLION COPIES is the summation of his hard-won publishing smarts. From filling orders to reducing risks to building a self-publishing venture into a profitable publishing business, readers can learn first-hand from this master marketer how to publish their own works-and profit handsomely from them.

Ted Nicholas, a successful author and independent publisher, has written 14 books on business and finance since his writing career began in 1972. Total sales of his books exceed 2.5 million copies.

HOW TO PUBLISH A BOOK & SELL A MILLION COPIES ($19.95 plus $4 S&H, 217 pages, 8 ½ x 11, soft cover, ISBN: 0-79310-620-6) is available at local bookstores or by mail order: The book can be ordered by calling Nicholas Direct, Inc, at 1 813 596 4966 or writing 19918 Gulf Blvd 47, Indian Shores, FL 34635

Loose inserts

A loose insert is a leaflet or small brochure that is inserted with another product, such as a bank/credit card statement or a newsletter. The advantage of a loose insert is the speed and the cost. For example, I could have my loose insert put in with 50,000 newsletters for far less than actually posting out a sales letter to 50,000 people.

On the whole, I would not sell directly from a loose insert; I would just give an overview and offer a free information pack by phoning in or returning the coupon.

How to circulate your loose insert

Firstly you write, design and print your insert and then you send it to the newsletter's mailing house; they then put your loose insert in with the rest of the mailing.

Most list brokers can help you with loose inserts and you can also contact the publication directly. The typical cost for a loose insert is around £100 per thousand.

Chapter 10

Back-end selling and good business practices

Let me make an important statement to you: A one-off sale will make you some money; however, a lifetime customer will make you very rich!

Here's the mistake that many businesses make, both large and small: Jackie Smith buys a book, video, or fishing rod from a company via mail order. Most companies fulfil that order and then that's it, they forget about the customer - BIG MISTAKE!

You see the chances are that as long as you have supplied a good product and you fulfilled Jackie Smith's order promptly, she will be happy with your company and in most cases would be happy to spend money with you again and again. In fact, you have now overcome the resistance of the first sale; she trusts you because you have previously delivered goods or a service to her.

How to correctly back-end sell

When you ship the client's first order, send a letter thanking them for their order and enclose a catalogue or details of another product that you think they will be interested in. I would also suggest that you send them a special discount voucher if they order from you again in the next 21 days. If you don't hear from them for a while, then send another letter stating 'You recently ordered the XYZ video from us and I would like to tell you about our new ZZZ video.'

And this is how you keep in contact with customers; alternatively, you could offer a newsletter, as we have previously mentioned. Some customers will buy everything that you send them details of - I know of a successful mail order entrepreneur that has mailed out 20 to 30 different product offers to the same customer and they have bought everything; in fact, it got to the point where he couldn't find anything else to sell them! Now imagine if he had just mailed out that client's first order and then forgotten about them.

Don't wait until the golden goose has died before you find another one!

Let's say that you have either developed or found a great mail order product. The orders are pouring in, everything's on the up and up and things are going great. Now most products don't sell forever - trends change, a competitor may start price cutting, etc. and before you know it, the golden goose is laying fewer eggs! The key is to have another product/service ready to roll out as it's rare that you will be able to sell the same product or service forever. As previously mentioned, you will need back-end products to make real money.

I do, however, want to warn you about a mistake that has been made by some people in this industry and that is dropping a product or pulling out of a business too early. It is important to let the winning products keep going until they start to become economically unviable, but make sure that you have something else up your sleeve or you have planned for a slow down.

Resting a product

If you have constantly been advertising a product, it can sometimes pay to put that project aside for a while and then bring it back again. Film-makers do this; recently the Titanic film has been brought back again and has been very successful all over again. Pop groups also do this; they go away for a year or two and then they come back with a new record or a greatest hits compilation.

Learn to watch trends

However big or busy you become, never allow yourself to get out of touch with what's going on, both in your industry, with technology, and any other up-and-coming businesses. You need to know what's going on in the world, what people are thinking, what they are buying and what they are concerned about. It is pointless burying your head in the sand when it comes to changes and new developments; you need to be ready to ride the wave of any trend, because if you simply ignore it, the chances are you'll get washed up! I have always liked to keep up to date with technology and the latest trends, and although it is impossible to know about every new product that comes on the market, you do need to have a good general overview.

Thanks to watching trends and taking advantage of new changes, many businesses have benefited greatly. For example, software like Quick Address, as previously mentioned, has enabled businesses to input data into the computer with better accuracy. By watching trends you position yourself in the right place.

The dangers of having too much money

If you're starting out with plenty of money to invest, you'd better watch out! Having too much money to begin with in business is worse than having a limited starting budget.

Let me explain: Many big companies and government bodies throw money at problems rather than finding an intelligent and non-costly way to avoid the problem in the first place. A large amount of start-up capital makes you lazy, complacent and comfortable. I started out with very little capital and many other successful business people also started out with a shoestring budget. This is the best way to start any business. Not having much money to spend will force you to investigate and research all the possibilities before you let go of that limited cash. Even if you do have a substantial amount of start-up capital, put it away where you can't get to it and force yourself to work within a tight budget, where every penny is crucial. You will make fewer mistakes by working like this than if you had an unlimited budget. Take for example, advertising agencies and their so-called wonderful adverts that they produce and place for big clients, like motor car manufacturers. I'm sure you've seen the double-page spreads which are a total waste of space. Anyone with half a brain could have produced a better advert in half a page or less! The reason the agency takes two pages is because it's the client's money and they have a big budget. FACT!

If you are starting out with a limited budget or are living in poverty, you should consider yourself lucky! Being poor is perhaps the best motivation for success. You'll have a real reason to make your project work. When you are broke you really don't have anything to lose, but have everything to gain.

Immigrants are four times more likely to become self-made millionaires

Although typically associated with the rags to riches story, a self-made millionaire is anyone who attains far greater success than his original circumstances would have indicated was possible. The self-made millionaires often have to overcome great obstacles to achieve their goals. They attain their success through education, hard work, and sheer willpower.

Sadly, too many people today believe that lounging on the shore, waiting for their ship to come in, constitutes the best pathway to reaching their goals. Instead, self-made millionaires throughout history have made their own way in life by reaching deep inside themselves and through willpower and elbow grease, creating their own destiny with the help of God. While there are always many factors to success, all are subordinate to work, which is the great key to success.

Here are a few examples of self-made people

Carlos Slim Helu

Forbes ranked Carlos Slim Helu as the richest person on planet earth since 2010. He was in third place before he leapfrogged Bill Gates and Warren Buffett to the coveted top place as the wealthiest person in the world. His wealth is estimated at US$69 billion as at March 2012.

He is one of six children, born to Julian Slim Haddad and Dona Linda Helu both Lebanese immigrants; on 28th January 1940 in Mexico City. The fact that he became fatherless at the tender age of 13 did not hinder him from obtaining a degree in Civil Engineering at the National Autonomous University of Mexico. Presently, he is the Chairman and Chief Executive of over two hundred companies in extensive industries including banking, telecommunications, road building, restaurants, etc.

Ralph Lauren

Ralph Lauren Polo trademark is a famous icon for elegance and luxuriance across the four corners of the globe. Ralph Lauren was born Reuben Lifshitz to Fraydl (Kotlar) and Frank Lifshitz both Ashkenazi Jews immigrants from Belarus; on 14th October 1939 in Bronx, New York. He changed his surname from Lifshitz to Lauren as he was been teased by his peers and it's easier to pronounce.

He was not born with a silver spoon in his mouth, his father was a poor house painter and his mother had hoped that he would become a Rabbi. Although he went to Baruch College for two years he later dropped out to follow his dream of entrepreneurship and fashion. He worked briefly as a salesman with Brook Brothers, later went to work for Beau Brumwell Neckwear, where he got his big break, he was allowed to design and sell his own brand 'Polo' ties in their store. The Polo ties were a hit with customers and other stores started selling them. As soon as he made enough money, he opened his own store which launched his passion and his career into the limelight. At present there are a total of 631 Ralph Lauren stores worldwide. In September 2012, Forbes estimated his wealth to be at US$6.5 billion. He is the 122nd richest person in the world.

Frederick Douglass 1818 – 1895

When it comes to rags and riches, there are no rags lowlier than those worn by American slaves. Rising from the shackles of slavery to extraordinary success required monumental amounts of hard work, tenacity, and passion. Frederick Douglas had these qualities in spades. Douglas understood that nothing in life would ever be handed to him on a golden platter. When his master's wife, who had been teaching him the alphabet, was reprimanded for doing so by her husband, Douglas continued to learn by interacting with white children and working through any written materials he could find. When he was traded to the cruel mastery of Edward Covey, who regularly whipped Douglas, he confronted his master, getting him to back down and never raise his hand to him again.

In 1838, Douglas took his greatest risk yet and escaped to Massachusetts. Douglas soon rose to prominence, becoming an outspoken abolitionist, a spectacular orator, a bestselling author and a newspaper publisher. During the 1888 Republican Convention, he became the first African-American to receive a vote to be nominated for presidency. Dying in 1895, Douglas had risen from slavery to become one of the most prominent and well-respected black men in the United States of America.

Nearly everything can start in a small way

Most people say that they need capital so they can start big and get ahead; well, I can tell you from experience that you are better off starting in a small way and building up. Here's a staggering fact: Sir Richard Branson of the Virgin Group owns 400 different companies including the airline, communications, etc. But did you know that apart from a few companies, each one was started up from scratch? They never buy an existing big business, they build them up themselves. His airline business was started on a very small budget with a couple of very old leased planes; it was then built up gradually and newer planes and routes were added. So the next time you think to yourself, if only I had more start-up capital, think again. You must stay **LEAN** and **HUNGRY.**

The Boss

Even when you are self-employed you still have a boss - the BOSS is the CUSTOMER.

"There is only one boss. The customer. And he can fire everybody in the company from the chairman on down, simply by spending his money somewhere else." Sam Walton, Walmart - one of America's most successful retailers

Remember that for most products and services the customer has a choice. No law states that he or she has to spend money with you or your company; it is your job to make the customer want to give their hard-earned cash to you. Too many of the big companies fail to recognise that if enough customers get fed up with their service and decide to stop using them, then it will only be a matter of time before a big company becomes a very small company!

Sam Walton's Pledge

If you or I went to work in a Walmart store we would be taught this important pledge:

"From this day forward, every customer that comes within ten feet of me, regardless of what I'm doing in this house, I'm going to look him in the eye, I'm going to smile, I'm going to greet him with a 'Good morning' or a 'Good afternoon' or a 'What can I do for you?' - so help me Sam!"

I suggest you copy out a slogan based on Sam Walton's for your business and stick it up on the wall and read it at least once a day.

Don't be an octopus

Do not spread yourself too thinly. Here are my four rules to remember when you start making it big:

1. Don't become complacent - that's how market leaders become second, third, or even worse.
2. Don't think that you know it all and that you are bulletproof.
3. Don't put it all back in. Remember the slot machines in Las Vegas - lots of people win, but most don't walk out with any money!
4. Don't think that you can do everything - you can't.

I've seen the octopus scenario so many times and I really want you to avoid making the same mistakes. I want you to be ambitious and to work to your full potential; however, I don't want you to become a gambler and be reckless. You and I are not bulletproof; if your business is a success then of course you may wish to expand and try other businesses; however, don't start trying to run 20 companies all at once - it just doesn't work. Now some people may say, 'But what about the companies that are conglomerates or people like

Richard Branson?' Well many conglomerates like Hanson Trust have recently demerged; they've gone back to being lots of smaller companies. As for Richard Branson, he mainly works on licensing his brands. For example, Virgin Cola is not made by him; it's made by another company and Virgin just brand the product. I also think that in time Virgin will go the Hanson Trust route and start demerging in the future.

Good ways to expand

Good ways to expand are with agents, licensing, joint ventures and subcontracting.

Agents

Recruiting an agent is a great way to have a large sales force to sell your products with no fixed cost; the agent only makes money when they make a sale. It's a win-win setup.

Licensing

Virgin and Disney are very good at this; they allow their names to be used on various products and in turn they get a cut. You can license or sell the rights to one of your products overseas.

Joint Ventures

Sometimes you don't want to take a big risk on your own or you may have expertise in one area, but you are lacking in another. That's where a joint venture can be a good idea, although obviously you have to pick your partner carefully.

On a smaller scale, you can do this with loose inserts, where you send out your sales material with others and vice versa.

At the moment, many companies on the Internet offer links/adverts to other websites and in return, they reciprocate.

Subcontracting/using a bureau

I heard of a guy who started a premium rate telephone business; he refused to lease his own lines, set up his own equipment and received a higher percentage per minute, but instead he opted for a bureau. He subleased the line, he used their machines and expertise, etc. and yes, he did receive a lower percentage per minute, but he didn't have any start-up costs or long-term contracts.

Sometimes it is better to take a smaller cut and not deal directly, especially if it's a sideline. Using an outside order-taking service is also a good example of subcontracting.

Are you ready for success?

Sounds like a crazy question but most people don't know how to handle success, money, and orders. Do you know that many companies go broke after they have received a big order? Well it's true; what usually happens is that they're just not prepared for the order - they have problems funding the stock and getting the staff to make up the orders and source the raw materials. They can't get the order out on time, they lose the order, and the company is left in a mess.

Let me give you some more problems that success in business can bring:

Stock problems

There will be times when you just can't meet the demand. My tips on dealing with stock problems are firstly, don't charge the customer's credit card or cash their cheque until you can deliver the stock. Secondly, tell the customer the TRUTH; explain that you really appreciate their business and patience and offer them a gift/small token as a thank you.

Administration

In business it is imperative to be organised and to have an effective administrative system in place, both manually and on your computer. An effective administrative system ensures that you can access files with ease. Bad administration means that you are out of control; if a customer phones you up to place an order or to check up on an order and you can't trace it within 30 seconds, then you're in big trouble.

Good filing

In most businesses, even with computers, you will still have some paper records. Make sure these are filed away in a good, logical order. If you are using a computer, then make sure that you co-ordinate the records on the computer with the paper records; for instance, account number 7450 on the computer should be the same as 7450 in the paper system. Don't let filing mount up; do it the same day as it's easier that way.

Good banking, accounting and security

Whether you are a Sole Trader or a Public Limited Company, you must get into the habit of good banking, accounting and security. The first rule is to always make sure you deposit your cheques every single day. Some people wait until the end of the week, which is not advisable; you should get the money into your account as quickly as possible. If you accept credit cards, then make sure that you go through their reconciliation procedure every single business day.

The second rule is accounting. You need to know exactly how much money you have in your bank account, how much is outstanding to you, if applicable, and how much you owe to others. Most people think that accounts, cash books and projections are not needed, but they are real management tools and they help you to spot problems quickly.

FACT: Banks make mistakes; let me tell you a few so you can watch out for them:

Cheques being cashed twice: The same cheque number, let's say 3456, for £3,900, appeared twice on your bank statement. Now if you don't spot it, that will be a big loss.

Bank Charges: You can use a few special services, e.g. a weekly statement, which you can get charged for. International payments can also be charged for - watch these charges carefully; look out for duplication and overcharging. The best way to eliminate this problem is to register for online access (which is free by the way) to your bank accounts so that you can monitor your income and expenditure 24/7. You can deal with any bank mistakes INSTANTLY and not a year later. I suggest that you have one for both personal and business accounts.

Accounting

If you don't have the patience for writing up columns, you can employ a bookkeeper; however, you would still need to know what is going on. You would need to look at the books and if there's something in there which you're not sure of, query it. You see, employing someone doesn't take the end responsibility away from you. Ensure that you understand the bookkeeping and accounting procedures, know the key dates of when taxes should be paid, etc. A good accountant will help you set up a bookkeeping and accounting system. The key to good accounting is to do it as you go along, not wait until the last minute.

Value Added Tax (UK) and Sales Tax (USA)

It will be very likely that you will have to register for VAT if you are trading in the UK and your turnover (not profit) is going to be over £77,000 per annum (for more information contact HM Revenue and Customs on 0845 010 9000 or visit their website www.hmrc.gov.uk/vat/start/register/when-to-register.htm#2).

By registering, you will have to add 20% (see note) onto the price of your goods, which is then passed on to HM Customs & Excise (normally every quarter) - basically you are collecting taxes on behalf of the government, which isn't really on , but you don't have a choice! The good news about being registered for VAT is that you can claim back the VAT which you pay on legitimate expenses in relation to your business. For example, you can go out and buy a computer for the business, which costs £1,000 + VAT, and you will be able to claim back the VAT.

Completing VAT returns can sound daunting; however, as long as you ensure that you keep good up-to-date records, then you'll find it quite easy after a while. Your local VAT office will help you and provides information for people who are new to VAT. Your accountant will also be able to help you set up either a manual or a computerised system for dealing with VAT. The main thing to remember is that the VAT money is not yours, even though it will be in your bank account for a while.

Security

Let me ask you a question: If your computer was stolen or caught fire, would you still be able to run your business? Most people don't think about this until it actually happens to them. You see, you need to have backup procedures, such as another computer in a different location with the same data stored on it and regular computer backups on a tape, disk or USB stick.

You see, if your computer is stolen, it's not the computer that is the real loss. It's the data stored on the hard drive, all your names and addresses, etc. which if you have backed up, can be restored onto a new computer and you can be up and running within minutes.

Fraud

It is important to keep your cheque books and other financial documents locked away. Even if you trust your staff, you have to think about visitors, such as couriers, delivery men, potential customers, sales representatives, etc. Beware that both small and large companies are victims of fraud, and don't fall for any scam letters from anywhere in world telling you that if you give them your bank account details, a letter headed piece of paper and your signature, they will transfer millions of pounds into your bank account - what will actually happen is that they will drain your bank account dry!

Beware of your rubbish

Ask any good investigative journalist how to find out anything about a person or a company and they will tell you to go through their rubbish. Make sure that you shred or rip up your rubbish; people throw bank statements, phone bills, utility bills and other letters away without even thinking. All these documents can be used against you in a fraudulent manner.

I remember there was a big story about Sarah Ferguson, Duchess of York; some years ago, she had written a note and thrown it away and the press had picked it out of the rubbish and printed it on the front page of the newspaper!

Bugging and espionage

Now you may be thinking, 'This girl is paranoid; why is James Bond 007 going to spy on me?' Well if you are in a competitive and sensitive business like software, finance, advertising, or mail order, your competitor could be watching you.

Here are some points to watch:

1. Can your computer screen be seen by someone from outside? At night, computer screens stand out. I have walked past many offices and I could see everything that was on their PC; with a long lens camera you could get clear photos of what's on your desk, wall or screen.

2. Are your telephones or offices bugged? It is possible that the free calculator gift that came through the post or the temporary girl that was helping you out may not be what you think!

3. Watch out for post interception, especially in offices where the post doesn't come straight to your door. Someone could pick up your post, steam it open, copy it, and seal it back up again and you wouldn't even notice. Just think, if you have just received a large contract or an order, the interceptor would now know all about it!

I have featured all these tips because I want you to be aware of what can happen. Like me, you will no doubt work very hard to achieve success and I would hate for something silly to cause you unnecessary problems and possibly large financial losses. You're going to find out that business is challenging enough, without any extra complications. JUST BE AWARE.

Doing business overseas

There's a BIG WORLD out there and the chances are that your winning product, video tape, or book, can be sold successfully outside your home country. It is a narrow view just to sell your product in the UK or USA or Guatemala because that's where your company is based. Today, with the Internet, reliable overseas couriers and cheap international fax and telephone rates, there is no reason not to do business in other countries.

If your product is a 'How to' manual, you could quite easily write a European edition and a US edition; some products will not even need to be changed. If you need help in selling overseas, you can possibly find an overseas agent or find a mail order company who will carry your product in their catalogue.

Credit cards are the global currency

Products can be sold to customers all over the world because with credit cards, there is no currency problem. A Visa card issued by a Spanish Bank goes through your terminal just as easily as a card issued locally. There are no currency problems because you get paid the amount you asked for, i.e. you still key in £35.00.

Do you think about overseas markets? If you advertise your products in an airline magazine or national newspaper, you will always receive enquiries from overseas - don't turn them away.

NOTE: Overseas freight and postage should be charged to the customer, as this can really eat into your profit margins. You may want to get a price list from the Post Office or your courier for various countries.

Chapter 11

Setting up your online business

Now as you know, more and more people today have become dissatisfied with their jobs and their pension provisions. So the interest in starting an online business has begun to increase. Yet many who look at such a project find it difficult to know where to start because of the mountain of information available on the subject.

However, during this chapter, I will help you to wade through the mountain of information available. This will, in turn, help you to decide on what is the right sort of online business for you.

One of the first things that you should bear in mind when setting up an online business of any sort, is that you must treat it as just that – a business. This means that you must be prepared to put in the time and effort in order to reap the rewards, even if you are only starting it as a part time venture at first.

Next, you must be prepared to invest some money into it. You do not need to put in large amounts, in fact, if you want, you could actually set it up on a very low budget. Also, what you should remember where an online business is concerned, the running costs are very low compared to a more traditional business.

However, the best place to begin is by picking what you like from the existing successful online business models already out there. So talk to others who have already made money in the niche that you have chosen, and then study, then implement the steps that they took to make it the success it is.

So now you need to think about just what sort of business it is you like to run. Some of the more popular types of online businesses to be found are: selling goods at auction sites such as E-bay, creating and then selling digital products (e-books are a good example of this) and setting up a custom storefront for your offline business. Also, you may want to make downloadable audio and video products for your customers, or you may just want to get into affiliate marketing instead. We will look at affiliate marketing a little further on in this chapter in a little more depth.

However, if you do choose to go with E-bay, one of the main advantages of setting up an online business based around this is as follows:-

- You will have immediate access to millions of customers.
- Plus you will have the opportunity to sell anything from cars to collectibles (e.g old sports cars).
- Also, setting up an account on E-bay is straightforward, and the costs relating to auctioning items on this site are extremely low.

However, it is important that you familiarize yourself with the site. So take a look at the different categories and auctions that are already taking place. Also check out their "How to Sell" section on the site.

For some, the thought of creating their own products seems very daunting, but if you happen to be an expert in a particular niche, then coming up with ideas should not be that difficult. It is important that you carry out some market research to make sure that people would buy related items.

So spend some time writing down or recording any thoughts that you may have with regard to the subject. Then go back and edit what you need, by putting things into a logical order. However, if you are someone who doesn't like writing, then take a look at some other sites selling those same products or similar ones and get ideas from them.

Make a note, if you can, of what is selling well and formulate some questions that someone who is interested in this product might ask. If you are able to find a friend who will do an interview with you, getting them to ask you the questions you have produced. You can if you want, record this interview and then make into an audio product which others can then download.

The next best way to make money with an online business is by selling someone else's products as an affiliate. As previously mentioned, we will look more closely at affiliate marketing later.

The best way of starting an online business is to do it in an area that you are knowledgeable or passionate about. This will help you to focus your attention, as well as help to create a small income more quickly. But over a period of time, you will soon develop new skills, and through persistence and patience, you will soon see some very good results appear.

The reasons for starting an online business

There are plenty of reasons as to why many people start an online business, and below I will provide you with just a few of them. For many people, the main reason that they decide to start an online business is to earn an extra income. Usually, this is in addition to the income that they are already earning. However for others, what starts as a part time venture, soon becomes a full time one. Another reason that people decide to start up an online business is that they have more control over their working life. Also, it provides them with a chance to spend more time with their family and friends. Today much too much time is spent working, and many people find that they have little or no time to spend with those that they love.

Furthermore, there are other reasons as to why so many people now choose to set up an online business.

Changed lifestyle

No longer would you need to get up in the morning to rush off to work and get caught up in all that traffic, or get sandwiched together like sardines in a tin on a train. Now that time which would normally be wasted sitting in traffic can be used to their advantage. Plus, it is up to you when you work, so if you don't want to start until late in the morning, you do not need to.

Prosperity

Because of the rapid advance in technology, many online businesses today tend to be prosperous, and so getting involved in this type of business is a good way to make some money.

Costs of Starting Up

This is probably one of the biggest reasons as to why many people choose to start an online business. As many of the transactions are completed online, there is little or no need for lots of paper and documents. What one really needs in order to get an online business going is a computer, a high speed broadband internet connection, printer, fax machine and few other essentials that an office may need.

As you can see, these are just a few good reasons for why setting up an online business might be the ideal choice for you.

Things To Consider Prior to Setting Up An Online Business

Let's look at things that you need to consider before you actually set up your online business.

What product or service will you want to provide?

For many people, they will start an online business based on knowledge and experience that they have already, while others may spot a gap in the market. But the most important thing that you can do is carry out research with companies and individuals that you do not know in order to get a more unbiased view.

Also, do as much reading and research on everything you can about particular areas of interest, as well as studying the pros and cons that this will have in relation to your overall goals. Plus, make yourself familiar with your competitors, as this will boost your confidence and enthusiasm for setting up an online business.

Where to work from?

You do not need to work from home, but most people with online businesses prefer to work from the comfort of their homes because there are no extra overheads like rent. But others may prefer to have an office away from the home, as they find it difficult to focus, as well as feeling isolated.

How to market the business?

It is important, if you want your online business to thrive, to ensure that you establish a web presence. The best way of doing this is by direct mail, networking, display advertising etc. But what approach works best for you will depend on the product that you are selling. The best way of finding out what will work, is by trying a different number of methods initially, and then go for it once you know which one is best. However, if you are unsure where to start, then look at how your competition is marketing their goods...if it works for them, it may work for you also.

Develop a Plan.

Without having a blueprint on how to reach your goals, you may find that not just your efforts, but the resources may well be squandered. Having a plan provides you with focus, direction and momentum to keep the business on track.

Check Laws and Regulations

It is important that you check to see if there are any local laws or regulations in relation to setting up an online business from home. Also, you will need to check laws and regulations in regard to being self-employed.

Setting up the Office

More often than not, an online business will be conducted from the person's home. So it is important that you set up a home office prior to starting up the business. You should arrange to have all the necessary equipment that you will need such as computer, internet connection, printer, fax machine (but not essential) are just a few things that you will need if you want to be successful with your online business.

Business Plan for an Online Business

By setting up a business plan, you are road mapping your way to success. It will help you to develop your business goals and strategies, as well as providing you with a better understanding of the marketplace. It will also highlight any business strengths or weaknesses that you may have, as well as providing you with an opportunity to take a close look at your competitors. If you want, you can also include financial projections, historical data and growth expectations into your business plan.

With any good business plan, it should show who the target audience is, and just how the product or service that is being provided will meet or exceed their needs and expectations.

When organising a business plan it is best if you break it down into sections such as:-

1. **Business summary** – The product or service you want to provide.
2. **Market analysis** – Research on the product or service and how the competitors are doing.
3. **Product positioning** – How to make it more prominent compared to your competitors.
4. **Market strategy** – How are you actually going to market it?
5. **Customer analysis** – Look at what the customer wants or needs.
6. **Financial analysis** – What you need to invest in order to set up the business and to keep it going while it is just getting started.
7. **Overall business goals** – What you hope to achieve in, say, a year's time.

But what is more important is that once a business plan has been developed, it should not lay in the back of a drawer somewhere. It should be a working plan that you can refer to when you need to. The best way to make a business plan is to keep it simple (one or two pages should be all you need). Certainly one of the best things you can do when starting an online business is to create a plan then stick with it.

Types of Online Business

We will look at some of the more common types of online businesses that people are running. Keep in mind the decision is really up to you as to what type of business you want to run online.

Marketing Business

This is one of the most common types of online businesses around. You can either run this business by exclusively marketing your own products, or by marketing those of other big budget companies. But this needs you to produce a visually striking web page that has all the necessary information and purchasing options on it for the products in question. In order for this business to be successful, it needs to be promoted effectively to potential customers via search engines, email or other sources.

Turnkey Internet Business

This is a very trendy type of business to have online. This is where you would purchase a website from an already established sector and then run the business on a web platform that is provided to you by the established business. In order to promote such an online business, there are many different methods that you could use, such as promoting individual products or services to your online customers.

Internet Services

This is a business where specific services are provided to online customers at a reasonable price. Such businesses are often set up according to a person's professional expertise and will provide services to their customers in relation to this. The types of businesses that will come under this umbrella are online consultancies, computer software assistance, and hardware trouble shooting and even such things as how to start an online business.

Medical & Health Care Facility Services

This is where someone will set up a complete online pharmacy and the services related to this type of business will be offered to online customers. Such businesses will provide customers with medical consultancy, selling of medications and other medical charges. If you look further into this line of business, you will find that there are several medical institutes who can franchise a person to run a virtual medical and health care facility for them.

But besides the ones mentioned above, there are many other kinds of online businesses around, such as entertainment websites, home decoration, Christian dating, article writing, fitness, allergies, online chat and interaction and email servers are just some. But no matter what type of online business ("niche") it is you decide to get involved in, it is important to plan carefully and have the ability promote the business professionally over the internet.

Steps to setting up an online business

The best way of setting up an online business today is as follows:-

- Choose a niche and then specialize in it. Do not think that you are going to make big bucks by selling everything under the sun (unless you are using E-bay, but even this is getting more competitive today).

- Choose or create a product. You can either use affiliate products or create your own.

  Probably one of the most important things to do when setting up an online business is to find a good name. It should be short, easy to remember and reflect what your business actually does. Your domain name is the name by which your online customers will remember you by. A good domain name is one that is memorable, short and easy to spell. There are many websites around offering domain names, and prices can start from as little as £1.29 (e.g. www.godaddy.com)

- Get your own website. Do not go for a free page on some affiliate site, but get your own. It is much easier to do than you think. Get some hosting (there are plenty of companies on the web today offering their services).

Then buy a template system if you cannot program (again take a look around the web and you will soon find plenty of companies offering web templates). Now all you have to do is start learning how to use it. However, if you are not technically minded then you will need to hire someone to handle all the technical aspects of your online business. This could include such things as building your website for you, the handling of your website hosting and the setting up of any domain names that you may require. A lot of businesses spend thousands of dollars to have a website built, thinking it needs all sorts of bells and whistles, but the fact is, most businesses do NOT need a complex and expensive website. Most businesses need nothing more than a 1-5 page website that tells people a little bit about their company and products, offers contact information, collects visitor details, and perhaps offers coupons or other incentives. You'll need to be certain your website is optimized for search engines. Just make sure you have phrases that relate to your business in page titles and content. It should also be professional and attractive so you can let potential customers know that your company can be trusted. If your website is poorly put together, it will give the impression that your company is shady.

Don't use Flash! Websites should be done in HTML/CSS, but Flash should be reserved only for minor visual elements. You want your site to be compatible in every browser!

- Always look for a secure and reliable host service provider. It is important that you examine the "uptime guarantee" that each service provider offers. Also, analyse the physical infrastructure of where your online business will be stored. But probably most important of all is that you should scrutinize the hosting providers "Back Up" and "Data Security" systems. This includes calculating how much time would be required to reinstall your online business if there was a complete infrastructure failure on the part of the hosting provider. This will help you to calculate the least possible loss to your business if such a situation arises. I have heard this statement from many successful internet marketers that 'The money is in the list' and I have found the statement to be very true. Building a list is important not only to get new customers, but also to keep existing ones loyal and happy. By building an email list, you can keep in touch with both current and potential customers, reminding them of the presence of your business, and hopefully to shop with you again! This means you need to get potential customers on your list, but also as many of your current customers as possible. You can have flyers, stickers, or business cards with your web address on them that you give to every customer who buys something from you. Make sure to point out that you will email special offers, announcements about new products or services and special events, and discounts and coupons from time to time. Offering discounts and coupons to your email list will keep them loyal and shopping with your company instead of your competitors!

Try http://www.aweber.com for easily setting up and managing an email list.

- Look at the ways in which you will handle the payments made by your customers. If you are selling an affiliate product, then this will not be a problem as the affiliate program will handle the payments for you. However, if you are selling your own product, then you will have to set up your own payment processing system. This will be looked at more closely later.
- Look at the ways in which you will arrange for goods to be delivered to your customer if selling your own products. You must look at local courier companies, as well as the postal service and find out which will be more cost effective for sending goods to

customers. Also, you will then need to decide on the pricing system for the sending of packages to your customer's. But it is important that you choose a shipping company who you know is going to be reliable. Look especially at those companies who offer an online tracking system.

Getting Traffic

SEO is one of the most popular buzz words in online marketing but unfortunately most marketers simply do not know enough about SEO to make this strategy work for them. Search Engine Optimisation, SEO for short is a technique to improve a web site's ranking in the search engines, to attract more traffic which in turn means more profit for you.

Many business owners think that online marketing involves setting up a website and waiting for the traffic to roll in, but things aren't that simple. In order for your website to really work for you, it needs to have a comprehensive marketing plan in place. That doesn't mean you need to spend thousands of dollars on an ad agency! You can easily do everything yourself.

Once you have a simple, attractive website online, it's time to start getting traffic to it. Most of your traffic will probably come from search engines, so you'll want to make sure you have important keywords in your page titles and content.

Let's say your company is an Italian restaurant in Madison, Wisconsin. Some potential keywords might be:

- Italian restaurant Madison Wisconsin
- Italian food Madison Wisconsin
- Italian restaurants in Madison
- Italian food in Madison

Those are just a few of the keywords you might want to use to help people find your site in the search engines. You'll also want to make sure your site shows up when someone searches for the name of your business, so you'll have to craft your page titles carefully.

An example for a page title might be:

Luigi's Italian Restaurant - Delicious Italian Food in Madison, Wisconsin

This way you would have your company's name (Luigi's), along with several keyword phrases (Italian restaurant, Italian food, and Madison, Wisconsin) in your title.

You would also want to make sure that those same keyword phrases appeared in the content of the page itself. For this reason, you want to be sure you your pages are mostly text rather than images or Flash.

For more in-depth information on SEO, visit www.genesismarketer.com to receive a free e-book called 'Advanced SEO Techniques – Turbocharge Your Traffic And Profits On Auto-Pilot!'

Directories

Another thing you will notice when you search for local businesses is that a lot of directories usually show up. For example, for my search "Italian food Madison Wisconsin", I see SuperPages.com, local.Yahoo.com, and MagicYellow.com, as well as a local directory called MadisonDining.com.

Since these sites all appear on the first page, you would definitely want to make sure your business was listed in all of them.

Always do a search for the top keywords for your business and make sure you get your company listed in every directory that shows up in the first two or three pages of results.

For more information on getting traffic, visit www.genesismarketer.com to receive 'Viral Traffic Generation – 21 Powerful Ways To Flood Your Site With Traffic!' free e-book.

Social Marketing

Many companies think social marketing wouldn't benefit them, and sometimes that's true. But if your major demographic happens to be under 40, social marketing is potentially a fantastic tool. Facebook and Twitter are both great for keeping in touch with your customers. Set up a fan page on Facebook and get your company a Twitter account. Then start adding friends by searching for people in your local area.

For more information on Social Marketing, visit www.genesismarketer.com to receive a free e-book on how to 'Dominate The Web 2.0 Market – Master The New Rules Of Online Marketing Success!'

How to Set Up an Online Business on a Budget

You have now decided to set up an online business, but your budget is very small, so how can you get going?

You could start off by looking for free domain names. Because there are so many companies around who are now selling domain names, the market has become quite competitive. But there are a few sites around that will register a domain for you at no charge. However, there is a catch with some of them in that they will set themselves up as the administrator for your domain and then only transfer ownership to you after a set period of time for free or will charge you a small fee.

If you are going to set up and launch a website, but do not want to pay the £5 a month that you can typically be charged for hosting, then don't. There are plenty of places on the web today that will host your site for free. But before you get too excited about this prospect, it is important to remember that there is a drawback from using such places. Most of these free host sites will place a banner at the top of your pages for allowing you to do this. However, there are some web hosts around who do not charge you a fee or force you to have a banner on your site either. While there are others who will remove the banners completely for a small fee each year, which is nothing compared to what you would pay to get someone to host your site for you each month.

What if you are someone who does not have their own product to sell, but still wants to make money online? Then look no further than becoming an affiliate marketer.

What is Affiliate Marketing?

Affiliate Marketing is a method of promoting a product in which an affiliate is then rewarded for every visitor, subscriber, customer and/or sale provided through their efforts to the actual company selling the product. The compensation or commission that an affiliate gets may be based on a certain value for each exposure, visit (pay per click), new customer (pay per lead), sale which is usually a percentage of the item sold (pay per sale or revenue share) or it may be a combination of any of these.

Many companies like to use affiliate marketing because they do not incur any marketing expenses unless the desired result is realised.

There are also some e-commerce sites around today which run their own affiliate programs, while others use third party services. These provide intermediaries who will track traffic or sales that are referred to them from their various affiliates. There are many businesses online today who owe much of their growth and success to the use of affiliate marketing. It has been especially successful for small and midsize businesses on the internet.

Why Become an Affiliate Marketer?

We have now looked at what affiliate marketing is, now let us look at some reasons as why it is a good type of online business to set up.

Advantages

- **No Production Costs**

With an affiliate program, production costs are no longer an issue as the product has been developed and proven to be good. Best of all, it has all come out of the merchant's accounts and not yours.

- **Little capital to set up.**

All you will need is a desk, computer, internet connection and word processing software to get started.

- **Free to join**

Normally it is free to join an affiliate program, and all the set up costs and shipping costs will be met by the merchant whose products you are selling. Plus, as you do not need anywhere to store goods, this is another reason for joining an affiliate program. So even if you happen to live in a 1-

bedroom apartment, you can still sell the biggest products going as an affiliate because all the goods are held by the merchant you are working as an affiliate for.

- **Choices**

There are thousands of products and services that you can choose from. So finding the right products for either a website you have already or one that you are planning to build is immense.

- **No need to have a Merchants Account**

This can be a time consuming and costly expense for anyone setting up a business for the first time. Certainly, it is even more so where an online business is concerned. However, as an affiliate, the merchant you are selling the product for will bear all costs, as well as handle the processing of all payments. So you never have to worry about any potential charge backs, fraudulent purchases or losing your merchant account completely as an affiliate. Plus, no longer will you be concerned with collecting and storing names and addresses of customers along with their credit card details, as this is all done by the merchant who you are affiliated to.

- **No customer service**

You do not need to worry about dealing with awkward or nasty customers and their complaints. This is down to the merchant to deal with.

- **Make money while you sleep**

Probably one of the best things about affiliate marketing is that you can make money while you sleep.

- **Minimal risk**

Another benefit to get into affiliate marketing is that if the product you chose isn't making money, then you can just dump it. Remove any links to the product and then start promoting another instead. This is because there are no long term contracts which bind you to selling one particular product, so the risk to you is minimal.

If you work hard at affiliate marketing, then the potential to earn a good income is high. It really depends on just how much you want it and how much effort you are willing to put in to the products you are trying to sell.

For an idea of just what kinds of products and services offer affiliate programs, check out JVZOO.com, Clickbank.com or ComissionJunction.com. These sites are generally at the very top of most affiliate marketers' lists.

For more information on Affiliate Marketing, visit www.genesismarketer.com to receive a free e-book called 'Become An Affiliate Marketing Master - How To Earn Big Profits Even If You Have No Products, No Website and No Experience!'

Using an Online Payment System For Your Online Business

There are many online payment services today which provide you with an alternative way to traditional payment methods. So unlike banks and credit card companies, services such as PayPal and CheckFree no longer require a business to have a merchant account. In fact, using services like this not only provides a quicker way for money to be paid online, but it is more secure than having someone sending you a cheque or cash. This is because the funds are electronically transferred to your account with them in order to settle any transaction made.

Such services have become especially popular among those who use online auction sites (such as E-bay), but also many other online businesses are now beginning to see the advantages of these services as well. However, what is important to know is how they work, and how to avoid any potential problems that may arise.

Such services use a relatively simple process in order to transfer money from one person to another. What you need to do is set up an account providing enough information which should include your real name, email address and credit card or bank account details (which are used to verify your identity). Then, in order for someone to pay you, they enter your email address and the amount of the transaction in question. This is then paid into your account, and can either then be transferred to your bank account, or a check can be sent to you.

However, many of the payment services will charge a small fee in order to transfer funds. For example, PayPal charges you up to 2.5% for each transfer that they make (but this all depends on the amount). But what should be remembered is that these fees are probably less than what you would normally pay for a credit card merchant account. Also, such services can be especially helpful when you need to arrange for small repetitive payments to be made to your account, such as affiliate rewards and commissions.

Drawbacks

But there are some drawbacks to be had from using a payment service, and these are as follows:-

- Many of them impose a daily or weekly limit on the amount of money that you send or receive. So if you want to exceed these limits you may find yourself incurring an additional fee for a "business account" or "premiere account".
- These services are not banks, and therefore are not subject to strict banking regulations or protected by Federal Deposit Insurance.
- Often these services provide their customers with less protection against fraud and abuse than many credit card companies offer.

- Also, they are sometimes quick to freeze a customer's account if they suspect fraudulent or other criminal activities are taking place. They can be so quick sometimes that some customers have found that their account has been frozen for no apparent reason whatsoever.

It is important that before you sign up to any payment service, you read through their terms and conditions thoroughly. Plus, also read through their terms of service agreement carefully. It is important that you fully understand and accept the service's dispute policy, limits on liability, their fee structure and any other rules or regulations that they may have. It is also important that you do not keep too much money in your account, rather hold in it enough to conduct a few days of business and any unused funds should be transferred over to your regular bank account.

Below are just a few more payment services that you may want to look at further when setting up an online business account.

- **Authorize.net**. This service processes credit card and checking account transactions.

- **PayPal**. This is probably the most well-known of payment services, and it allows user to user payments. This is where a payer uses a debit or credit card to pay money into another user's account. Or, in fact, they can use money they already have in that account in order to pay for the goods they have purchased.

- **WorldPay**. This service provides both an internet merchant account, and payment processing service in one package.

Marketing Your Online Business

We will look at various ways in which you can market your online business. The reason for marketing an online business is in order to get that all important traffic to visit your site. This traffic consists of visitors, who will then become your customers and start purchasing your product or service from you.

The first thing you need to do is learn how to optimize your website so that it will start getting ranked in the top three search engines (Google, Yahoo and Bing). The sooner you do this the faster it will get ranked and the sooner the traffic will start to appear at it. A great way of doing this is by investing in either a book, on how to optimize your site, or you could try some of the following methods instead. The best way in which you can optimize your website is by ensuring you have back links to your site. This is where you have links to your site placed on other sites through various different methods. These methods are discussed below:

- **Link Exchanges**

This is where you exchange links with other websites that have complementary products or services to your own. It will not only give you direct traffic from the link, but will help to increase your pursuit for getting ranked higher in search engines.

- **Write Articles**

It is important that the articles you write are interesting and full of useful information regarding your niche. This is probably one of the best ways around for gaining more traffic to your website. Not only is it free, as there are many article sites around where you can have your articles published for free, but each article you have published will be providing a link back to your site. This means that you are helping to gain even higher rankings where search engines are concerned. When writing an article, you should always include information about you, the author (this will usually be in a resource box at the bottom of your article), and do not forget to include that all important link to your own website.

By distributing to numerous article sites, you are not only gaining traffic (as when someone sees it on there, they will click on your link if they like what they saw), but also you get a link that points directly back to your site, which the search engines use to rank sites. However, if you are someone who dislikes writing, then you could always look at using a Ghostwriter. There are many sites around today who offer ghostwriting services, but when initially setting up an online business, this may not be an expense that you want to incur.

- **Online Forums**

When using these, do not forget to include your signature line at the end of any comments that you make, as this will then provide a further link back to your site. The best bet is to stick to forums that are on the same topic as what you are trying to sell. Not only will you be learning about your potential customer's desires, but you'll be able to establish yourself as an expert in the field.

- **Blogs**

Blogs are a great way of ensuring you get back links to your site. So why not start a blog on your website? But ensure that you post to your blog several times a week and think of it as news page for your site. Certainly blogging has become the in thing at the moment on the web. You only have to do a quick search to find out just how many there are.

For more information on blogging, visit www.genesismarketer.com to receive a free e-book on how to blog for cash.

Conclusion

What you should remember is the costs of running an online business are considerably reduced. This is because you do not actually need an office, you can work from home. No need to employ others and all you need to get started is a good computer and good internet connection.

But there are some problems that you do not get with a traditional business, such as hackers, viruses, websites going down and data preservation.

However, the most important aspect of any online business is to generate traffic to your site. There is no point in you having a great product if nobody knows about it. So get a strategy in place which will generate the traffic required to bring in those important visitors, and then sales to your site.

So the best way of starting any kind of online business is to sit down and write up a plan. Once you have done this, then you can start looking at all the steps that have been discussed earlier.

Marketing your business online is a lot simpler than most business owners believe. All you need is a simple website, a little initiative, and a few hours to get everything set up.

You can literally have your entire marketing system online and in place in just a few hours, and it will be more effective than you ever expected!

Here's a checklist you can use to get started:

- Get a simple website online. 1-5 pages is usually plenty.

- Submit your site to Google's local business search.
- Be sure to include keywords in page titles and content.
- Submit your site to local and national directories.
- Use Facebook, Twitter, Stumble-upon, Pin-interest,
- Build and manage an email list.

There are many books on the topic of online business. I have found a free online information website which is geared towards newbies, intermediate and experienced online marketers. For more in-depth information into how to set up and run a successful online business please visit www.genesismarketer.com to get hold of 7quality free e-books. The e-books are follows:

1. Advanced SEO Techniques – Turbocharge Your Traffic And Profits On Auto-Pilot!
2. Maximum Profits with Private Label Rights – Everything You Need To Know To Transform Your PLR Into Cash Machines!
3. Become An Affiliate Marketing Master - How To Earn Big Profits Even If You Have No Products, No Website and No Experience!
4. Viral Traffic Generation – 21 Powerful Ways To Flood Your Site With Traffic!

5. Dominate The Web 2.0 Market – Master The New Rules Of Online Marketing Success!
6. Super Joint Venture Secrets – Proven Tactics For Getting Top Joint Venture Partners To Promote For You!
7. Blogging For Cash – Simple Secrets To Turn Your Computer Into A Cash Machine!

Chapter 12

Tendering for public contracts

The public sector spends £220 billion in the UK each year and, because their buying needs are very large, lots of different kinds of businesses sell products or services to them. Even very small businesses can benefit from public sector procurement – 16% of all the businesses that have ever won European Union contracts have nine employees or fewer.

The public sector is made up of organisations such as central and local government and their executive agencies. The public sector buys a huge variety of products and services and provides a customer base that is stable and pays on time.

The work the public sector is looking to place is offered through contracts and tenders. You can find public sector tenders on various websites and tender alert services. There are strictly defined procedures that have to be followed.

FINDING CONTRACTS

Public sector organisations are legally obliged to release tenders for works and services. In the majority of cases these are listed on their websites and traditional print media. Electronic procurement and tendering systems or e-procurement are also increasingly prevalent.

A number of companies provide subscription alert services which send notifications of relevant tender documents to the subscriber. An array of private organisations also assist businesses in finding out about these tenders. Cost may vary from a few pounds a week to a few hundred.

Because of the special language and sometimes difficult-to-grasp procedures, some organisations also offer companies tender writing training, or do the writing for them.

Official Journal of the European Union (OJEU)

The main source of information about European Union (EU) public procurement is through the OJEU.

Tender Electronic Daily (TED)

Tender Electronic Daily (TED) is the online version of the *Supplement to the Official Journal of the European Union* dedicated to European public procurement. All public sector contracts worth more than the value set in the EU procurement directives must be published in Tenders Electronic Daily (TED), the daily supplement to OJEU. This provides information on the current requirements and invites suppliers to express an interest, or to tender directly in some cases. It also sets out information about contracts that have been awarded.

How you can benefit from TED

TED provides free access to business opportunities. It is updated five times a week with approximately 1500 public procurement notices from the European Union, European Economic Area and beyond. You can browse, search, and sort procurement notices by country, region, business sector and more.

Information about every procurement document is published in the 23 official EU languages. All notices from the European Union's institutions are published in full in these languages.

Why you should register on TED

- To access the entire content of TED, including the archive.
- To personalise search profiles, according to your needs.
- To get email alerts based on your search profiles.

- To personalise RSS feeds for your websites and RSS readers.
- Registration and usage of TED is absolutely free, and will remain so.

www.ted.europa.eu
www.enterprise-europe-scotland.com
www.contractsfinder.businesslink.gov.uk

The Public Sector contract opportunities available

Public sector organisations include Transport for London (TFL), National Health Service (NHS), Ministry of Defence (MOD), Her Majesty's Prisons (HMP), Metropolitan Police, schools, colleges, universities, museums, art galleries, local councils, fire brigades, etc. They need to buy goods, services, and expertise in the same way as any organisation does. Working with the public sector means that you have a long-standing, stable customer who must pay their bills within the agreed credit period.

Key areas that most departments buy goods and services for are:

- IT hardware, software and services
- office furniture and equipment
- temporary and permanent staff
- cleaning and maintenance services

- construction work, painting and decorating
- motor vehicle management and parts

Specialist departments will buy specific skills and services relevant to their function; for example, the NHS will purchase healthcare equipment and professionals' services.

The Public Procurement

Public procurement is the process by which government departments or agencies purchase goods and services from the private sector. Governments, regional and local public authorities, or bodies governed by public law, use this process in order to obtain goods and services with taxpayer money.

The Procurement process

Stage 1 Identify Procurement Needs The need to procure arises as a result of the expiry of an existing contract, or as a result of the completion of a best value review or as a result of a desire to improve service levels and efficiency.
Stage 2 Expression of Interest Notification

This is when you formally respond to an advert and you are expressing an interest in tendering for the contract.
Stage 3 Pre-Qualification Questionnaire (PQQ) This is your first chance to impress your potential client. You are likely to be asked to provide the following information: • Basic details of your organisation • Financial information • Business activities • References from previous clients • Insurance details • Details of any recognised quality management certificates • Copies of your health and safety, equal opportunities and environmental management policies • Professional and business standing of the organisation and its directors/trustees, e.g. details of any criminal records or bankruptcies • Examples of relevant experience in the service area of the contract • First indications of how you propose to deliver the service

Stage 4 Select Tender List After the receipt of the pre-qualification questionnaire, the authority will score each section of the PQQ and only those companies that score the highest will be invited to progress to the next stage of the process. These are the companies that will be sent INVITATIONS TO TENDER.
Stage 5 Invitation to Tender This is the procedure for generating competing offers from different bidders looking to obtain an award of business activity. This is usually preceded by a pre-qualification questionnaire (PQQ).
Stage 6 Tender Submission The purchasing organisation will require that you submit your bid by the closing date. If your submission is late, you will most likely be rejected.
Stage 7 Tender Evaluation Tenders are often evaluated in two stages, and quite often by separate groups. First there is a technical stage, to ensure the product or service will meet the specification and performance requirements; then the commercial evaluation

stage. Only tenders that comply with specifications and general requirements will be considered for acceptance. If a tender does not meet requirements it will be treated as invalid.
Stage 8 Contract Award Once the procuring organisation has made a decision on who to award the contract to, it will communicate its decision to all the tenderers. The successful tenderer will normally receive an official purchase order or other formal notification of the procuring organisation's intention to award a contract.
Stage 9 Contract Start The beginning of the contract management phase.

How to bid for public sector contracts

There are many ways you can increase your chances of putting in a successful bid for a public sector contract.

Tips include:

- **Matching tender opportunities with your core business capabilities**

This may mean filtering or refining the tenders you have received to achieve the best match between the client's requirements and your capabilities.

Remember – there are over 9,000 different tender categories.

- **Thorough examination of your tender notices**

Read your tender notices carefully and look for clues in terms of what the client's requirements and expectations really are. Be aware of any mandatory requirements and be sure you can meet them, e.g. health and safety policies, quality procedures, minimum turnover, and staff required to possess certain key qualifications. If in doubt, contact the client and ask.

- **Pre-qualification Questionnaire (PQQ)**

Many organisations inviting tenders will expect you to complete a pre-qualification questionnaire. Make sure you accurately answer all the questions. Remember that the Invitation to Tender stage will be based on the information you provide on the pre-qualification questionnaire (PQQ).

- **Understand and be realistic about your capabilities**

Be realistic about the limitations of your business and how much you can deliver. Do not embellish or exaggerate your capabilities as you will be asked for references and proofs. Consider this from the client's perspective, how they will view the facts and figures that you will be required to provide about your business. Review this information carefully. Be honest and ask yourself questions. Are there potential gaps or weaknesses in your capabilities? If so, consider discussing these with the client before submitting. This will save you money and time. Also, estimate the costs of fulfilling the contract and your potential profit to see if it is worthwhile bidding.

- **Collaboration**

If you think there is a real possibility that your bid might be discounted (perhaps because your firm is too small or doesn't have the full complement of skills required) but does possess a strong capability in one of the key areas of the bid, then why not consider a joint bid with another business whose skills/experience complement your own?

- **Know when not to bid**

The bravest decision is sometimes not to bid for a particular tender if you feel your business may possess weaknesses in some key areas. Also, estimate the costs of fulfilling the contract and your potential profit to see if it is worthwhile bidding.

There will always be other tenders that better match the all-round capabilities of your business.

With some tenders your best chance of success may lie in being a second-tier supplier to the winning bidder.

- **Contract Awards**

Becoming a second-tier supplier to the winning company also means avoiding the tendering process altogether. You may simply be required to provide a straightforward quote for the product or service required. A Contract Award Notice will tell you which company has won the tender you are interested in.

- **Deadline**

Procuring organisations have strict deadlines and being five minutes late may mean all your hard work goes to waste. Note the day, date, and time by which the tender must be submitted. Make arrangements in advance for delivery (post, courier, etc.).

Summary

Pre-qualification

There may be a number of pre-qualification stages that you may be asked to go through before being invited to submit your tender. Public bodies will ask for references, as well as information on your current financial position and previous experience.

All responses are evaluated and will form the basis of deciding whether you will go through to the next stage.

Submitting the tender

The tender is your opportunity to show that you are the best supplier for the job. The public sector looks for the 'best value for money' - a combination of cost and the optimum ability to meet the contract's requirements. You should complete the tender documentation carefully, making sure you prove that you can provide this 'best value' and show how you would intend to do it.

You may also be required to prove that you meet standards for quality assurance, equality and diversity.

- Investigate your sector and only bid for work that you can deliver.
- Plan and cost the full extent of delivering the contract to ensure that you have taken full account of overheads and given due consideration to all the resource implications.
- Make sure you know early on in the procedure, what format you will have to use to fill in the buyer's documents. You also need to know what timescales you are working to and whether interviews will be likely.

- Always provide the information you are asked for. If you cannot do so, check whether your bid will be acceptable before you send it back. If you are not sure of anything, ask the buyer in good time.
- Make sure you accurately answer all the questions.
- Remember that at the Invitation to Tender stage you are being evaluated on how well you would be able to deliver the goods or services required, in line with the criteria given.
- Plan your bid around the timetable the buyer gives you to make sure you can meet all deadlines.
- Remember, your bid will be evaluated only on the information you provide as part of the tender process.

Chapter 13

Learning to invest in your business and keeping costs down

When you start making money in business you will no doubt start focusing on things that you may want to buy for your business and I would like to share some of my experiences:

1. I believe in investing in computers and machinery that will be of benefit to your business; however, I believe that anything you buy for your business must earn its keep - I am not into buying something just to look good.

2. If you need to buy a machine, think about the possibilities of maybe renting one first, or taking it on a trial basis. Also, would it be cheaper to subcontract the task out to another company or to use a bureau?

3. If you are tempted to move into business premises just because you are doing okay, then think again. Save your money, work from home and use a business centre.

4. Try to always buy a slightly used/ex-demo or even a slightly older model (see saving money section for more tips).

5. Always keep your costs down to a minimum. Many people who start to make money get complacent; they buy items that they don't need, they start taking expensive business lunches, taking out vanity advertising or features about their business and generally buy office items at inflated prices. Remember, it is easier to save £1 than it is to earn £1.

I read that Henry Ford offered $25,000 (and that was a very big sum in those days) to anyone who could show him how to save a single nut and bolt on each automobile he made. It was thanks to Henry Ford's penny-saving schemes that cars were able to be produced at a price where nearly everyone could afford to buy one. Think about this example when you are running your own business. In the long term you would be able to save thousands of pounds in your business, which in turn means extra profits for you, just by saving small amounts here and there. Costs such as envelopes, postage, and paper, which most companies don't even think about, can lead to massive savings.

NOTE: If you work for a company or you shop/do business with someone and you spot something that they could be doing to save money, then write to them, giving them a rough idea. Then if they are interested, which everyone will be, get a solicitor to draw up an agreement and sell them the idea. Something simple that you spot could be worth thousands of pounds to you.

The saving money section will give you more ideas on keeping your business costs down. When people start out in business they tend to be very resourceful because in most cases they have very little capital; then when they start making money, they become complacent and wasteful - don't make this mistake. Now at the same time, don't be a total miser; ensure that you are comfortable when you are working; have a nice chair, a few pictures and maybe some plants, etc. A happy work place makes you more productive.

Investing wisely in business is essential. I have already mentioned that I invested in a computer and a laser printer as soon as I had my first profits. Companies who don't invest in machinery and technology get left behind. I've seen companies that have clapped-out old machinery which breaks down all the time, yet the directors have brand new company cars! You need to get your investment priorities right.

Why do companies go broke?

First of all, if you follow everything that I have told you till now, you will avoid all of these problems. It is quite amazing that I had addressed all of these problems before I read the following research. The researchers at the Imperial College of Science, Technology and Medicine carried out a study a while back, about why small and medium sized businesses fail. They sampled 486 businesses which had failed and concluded as follows:

1. Failure to clearly target the product or service at the right customer was often a contributing factor of failure. (Remember what I was saying about sending out direct mail to the wrong people.)

2. Underpricing, with businesses not realising that their market would have been prepared to pay more for their product or service. This was more of a problem than overpricing. (Remember what I said earlier - it is always better to overprice than underprice, and new businesses normally underprice.)

3. Lack of planning was a frequent cause of failure, especially for new businesses. (I would guess that they were not ready for success.)

4. Poor management was also common, along with poor financial systems, failure to manage debt, and poor planning (again, you may have thought I was bonkers when I said earlier that I always knew how much money was in the

bank and how much was outstanding). I also doubt that they had written personal or business goals.

The survey also concluded that many business owners didn't see that their business was getting into trouble until it was too late; they were also reluctant to seek any outside help.

Learn from these business failures and you can avoid these deadly mistakes; ignore them and you'll be another statistic!

Attending trade shows, public events and large shopping centres

I have attended many trade shows and shows aimed at consumers, such as the Ideal Home Exhibition, and it is always a good place to look for new contacts and ideas. It is thanks to attendance at trade shows like this that many people have conceived ideas and have been able to make money.

You should be aware that you can make large amounts of money by selling products at trade shows, especially if your product has a general appeal. This is also a good way to test products and get instant market reactions. One of my heroes in sales and business is Ron Popeil, who is a multi-millionaire, thanks to his business, Ronco. He started his career by working on market stalls and then by selling his products at exhibitions and shows. Ronco's products included pasta-making machines, food slicers, the 'Food Dehydrator', and the 'Pocket Fisherman', to name but a few. Now when Ronco went on to television, he used many of the techniques that had been tried and tested from his live demonstration days.

Tips on making a trade/public show work for you

1. Identify the target audience - will they be interested in your product? It is pointless attending the Clothes Show Live Exhibition if you are selling a product relating to cars!
2. How many people attended the show last year/last time?
3. When booking a stand, try to get the best position you can, even if it means paying a bit extra, because location is important, not the size of your booth. Good locations are near to toilets/rest rooms and snack areas.
4. Have a practice run at home. Set up the booth with the exact space that you will have at the show; this will give you an idea of how you can set up the booth with the maximum effect.
5. Make sure that at least one or two other people are there to help you run your booth.
6. Make your booth look as professional as possible. Use posters and display your product

clearly - people need to know exactly what you are selling. If your product can be demonstrated, then make sure you do so; have a microphone and make as much noise as you can - you need to attract the audience's attention. Don't just sit there like a lemon; try to build up a crowd. People are like a sheep and will soon flock around you.

7. Keep the price of your product at a round figure when you're at a show; this makes it easier for people to pay in cash without giving any change, i.e. £10 or £20. Shows are one of the only places where you can make money with lower profit margins, because the volume is big and you don't have any direct mail or postage costs.

8. Have a jar where people can drop their business cards in, or fill in a slip with their name and address to receive further details. You can build up great mailing lists at shows. You could hold some sort of free draw/raffle to encourage people to give their details.

9. Have plenty of bottled water and a few snacks on your stand; it will be a very long day and you need to drink. Also, the chances are that you are going to be on your feet all day, so wear comfortable shoes.

10. Be ready for anything: bring sticky tape, scissors, pens, markers, paper, and cardboard, so that you can make up any last-minute

signs. Also remember to have a cash box to put all the money in!

Summary

Selling products directly at a trade show or public exhibition can be a great way to make large amounts of money in a few days. Your main cost is the stand, but if you have the right product for the market, then you'll make money. If you are new to trade shows you will want to start off by testing a few of the smaller shows before you go for the big ones.

Making trade shows/exhibitions work without paying to exhibit there

The key to this is to bring lots of business cards and leaflets about your product or service and give them out to as many of the exhibitors as possible. Let's say that you sell to engineering companies; now for you to visit 400 different companies, possibly all over the world, would be very expensive, yet by attending a major trade show where these companies will be exhibiting, you can go from stand to stand. Try to pick the quietest day of the show, normally the morning of the last day; this way you will get more time.

Chapter 14

Summary to making money

I want to use the next few pages to summarise and recap. The keys to making money are:

1. Be in business for yourself

Whether it is part-time to start with, or by acting as an agent, or consulting a few customers alongside your existing job, start your own business.

2. Put the customer first

The aim in business is of course to make money; however, if you just focus on the money without taking any time and effort to look after your customers and to find out what the market wants, then it is going to be very hard to make money. You must also genuinely enjoy your work, be proud of your business and be happy to serve your customers. Some of the world's most successful entrepreneurs, such as Henry Ford, Conrad Hilton, and Soichiro Honda, always believed that money was just a by-product of their business. Realise that a one off sale/order will not make you rich - it is repeat business that will make you rich.

3. Be market driven, not product driven

Find out what the market wants or who you can sell the product to before you start to spend time and effort on making/buying a product.

4. A one man/woman company must still give a professional image

Using good letter headed paper, having a good telephone manner, computers, a business centre and a fax line will put you on a level footing with the big boys, even though you are a tiny company.

5. Learn not to waste money

Don't get suckered into wasting money in business; negotiate everything and run a tight ship, even when things are going well. At the same time, realise that money invested wisely to improve the business (money spent on training books, seminars, etc.) is money well spent - it's pointless using Stone Age equipment and not investing in new skills.

6. Be ready for change and be prepared

One thing is certain in business and that's nothing is certain in business. Things change; today's big seller is tomorrow's totally unfashionable item. Keep your eyes open, watch out for new trends and markets. Also be ready for problems, such as computer failures etc.

7. Don't quit, believe in yourself, work hard and give everything your very best effort

You must realise that stress, problems, new challenges, frustration and let-downs are part of everyday business life and if you are going to start sulking and hide in a corner when something goes wrong, then you won't survive in business for very long. Understand this: you will get knocked down. It happens and it's acceptable; the question is, do you keep bouncing back up again? You must bounce back, learn from your mistakes, and keep going. Stay on the ground for too long and that's where you'll be forever. Get up, fight back and you'll be a winner.

8. Realise that marketing is the key

'No enquiries means no orders, no orders means no money, no money means no business, no business means you're out on the street!' Vince Stanzione

I know this sounds harsh but that's the reality - good marketing makes or breaks you. You must advertise, use press releases, use direct mail, use the Internet and any other method you can that will effectively spread the word about your product or service.

My closing advice on making money

In short: be in business for yourself. It can be lonely at times and the hours can be long, especially when you are starting out, but the benefits both financially and personally of owning your own business, far outweigh the few disadvantages. The sense of pride that you get is hard to describe until you feel it yourself; starting a business from nothing and building it up with your own efforts, blood, sweat and tears is a sensational experience. You can never get the same satisfaction from working for someone else.

Remember that this section is just the beginning; to succeed in business you will need to become a good student, as you will need to continually learn new skills and information. This book will get you started, however, there's a long road ahead, but it's one worth travelling on.

The information I have revealed in this book will allow anyone with little or no previous business experience to start making money the smart way. I've given you tips that will save you making the mistakes that most business start-ups make and by using this information, together with your own hard work, perseverance, and with the help of God, you will be a winner in business in Jesus' name.

In the next section we will talk about saving money and how to get 'the maximum bang for your buck'. Being a smart buyer and making your money go as far as possible is an important factor which is often overlooked in business.

Chapter 15

Saving money

Now I want to reveal to you the power of saving money and being a SMART BUYER.

When I say to people that shopping and buying is difficult they think I am exaggerating; after all, when you see something that you or your business needs/likes, you buy it. Yes, you can do that, but if you want to hold on to your money and maximise your spending power, then you need to be a smart buyer.

I've seen many people struggling to live on £100,000 a year and then I've seen people who have everything they want on £100,000 a year, so what makes the difference? It's the way the money is spent.

Making every £1 equal at least 150 pence

Once you learn to get 'the maximum bang for your buck', you will realise that instead of having to work harder to make more money, you can simply spend wisely and still achieve the same results. Now, I'm not saying that we should go and live rent-free on a park bench to save money! That's not a lifestyle that you or I would aspire to have, however, I am talking about how simple actions that most people don't think of or are too embarrassed to ask for, can make a massive difference.

So let's get started on the real ways to save money...

Money Saving Expert Website

MoneySavingExpert.com is a British consumer finance information and discussion website founded in February 2003 and owned by financial journalist Martin Lewis, with the aim of providing information and journalistic articles to enable people to save money. I and some million others have found www.moneysavingexpert.com to be comprehensive and useful when it comes to making an informed decision. It covers information on almost everything: tax benefits, travelling, credit cards, how to claim free shopping vouchers, mortgages, loans, etc. I have found the website to be a one-stop shop for everyday living issues and best of all, the information is free of charge. The website was recently sold in June 2012 to its rival, Money Supermarket, for £87m.

The Money Saving Expert website consists of 4 key tools:

- Weekly Money Saving Email

Martin's Free Money Tips email is sent to over 7 million people every week and contains a mixture of editorial articles and the best current tips from users in the site's forums.

- Money Saving Best Buy Guides & Articles

The main site has a large variety of articles, from childcare vouchers to cheap contact lenses; balance transfers to boots bargain hunting.

- Money Saving Tools

Money Saving Expert creates and hosts their own price comparison tools, including the Flight Checker, Premium Bonds Calculator, Call Checkers, De-motivator, and the Budget Planner.

- The Money Saving Forums

The site has forums, with over 26 million posts, to discuss matters related to money in general (including loans, benefits, debt, shopping, etc.), as well as a few forums for general chat.

Airlines

Many people often fly around the world for such small fares and the simple answer is, they go looking for the best deals. Now I have been told that I'm not allowed to name any airlines but I will you give some examples and ideas.

Don't buy the ticket direct

The biggest mistake you can ever make is to phone an airline's Freephone central reservations number - only fools do this. You'll never get a discount by dealing directly - why? Because most airlines don't want to be seen offering discounted flights. Instead, they sell their leftovers or X amount of seats to travel consolidators, who then sell the fares at a discount. The only time you should ever phone the airline directly is to use them for information, flight times, and to get a starting price.

NOTE: I have been able to get a discount on every major airline, even when I have been told by the airline that they do not discount!

A friend of mine went to Canada with a large airline and travelled first class for the price of an economy ticket! It's amazing; she paid £500 for this ticket, yet on the ticket it said £2,800 and no doubt people on the same flight were paying this amount. She booked the ticket through a consolidator, not directly through the airline. Now of course, when she was on the plane she was treated as a full fare customer - the cabin crew didn't know what price she paid for the ticket. She's a smart shopper and this is one of the ways I would recommend to make your money go further.

Getting upgrades

On many occasions I pay the lowest economy fare and again, I do this through a consolidator. The key to getting an upgrade is to look presentable, be friendly, confident and generally be a nice person to do business with. Remember what I told you at the start of the book about 'taking an interest in the little people', well here's where to do it.

The main reason I get an upgrade is because I ask for one - it's simple isn't it? If you don't ask for an upgrade, you can't expect the booking clerk to say, 'Here, have a First Class seat!'

Tips for upgrades:

1. Join their frequent flyer programme. It's normally free and it shows that you are a loyal flyer. Collect as many as you possibly can from different airlines.

2. Look smart. Many airlines will not upgrade you if you are wearing jeans etc. You need to look the part if you want to travel in business or first class - don't look like a tourist, wearing a t-shirt with a camera round your neck!

3. Say that you would be grateful for a 'courtesy upgrade'. If it's your birthday, honeymoon, spouse's birthday or a special occasion, ensure that you tell the check-in clerk this; people like to help out if it's a special occasion. Even if you don't get an upgrade, most airlines will give you a treat, e.g. a box of chocolates or a gift.
4. Buy a few shares in various airlines. This way you can say that you're a shareholder and in turn you actually own part of the airline. It might only be ten shares, but you are still a legal voting shareholder. Some airlines offer special rates for shareholders.

Good Consolidators

Here is a list of consolidators that I swear by for both business and economy class. Now before I go any further, I want to state that I receive no commission or have any incentive to recommend these companies; myself and others have used them and I have found that they offer a good service at good rates. Like all things in life, companies and offers change, so you will still need to do your own research and seek out your own consolidators.

NOTE: Don't confuse a consolidator with a high street travel agent; most travel agents are not much better than direct airlines.

www.flight4.com
www.flight4.co.uk
Flights price comparison website:
www.momondo.co.uk
Website: www.eConsol.com contact number: 0207 312 1730
Website: www.teletickettravel.com contact number: 01293 555 708 or 0843 2081 246
Website: www.skylordtravel.com contact number: 0208 582 1199

JTA Travel Group,
227 Church Road,
Yardley, Birmingham,
UK, B25 8UR
Website: www.traveljta.co.uk
Contact number: 0121 508 5555 or 0844 9840 800

Airline Network Plc
Headquarters
The Trident Centre
Port Way
Ashton-On-Ribble
Preston
Lancashire
Tel: 01772 333 600 or 0844 692 6787
Fax: 01772 760 287
www.netflights.com

Booking and paying for your flight

I always pay using a credit card; this way, should anything go wrong, then it's the credit card company's problem and not yours! 99% of agents and consolidators are reputable; however, there are a few rogues who will try to sell you a worthless ticket.

Note: A debit card or a charge card is not the same as a credit card and does not give you the same rights.

Hotels

At some time or the other we all stay in hotels, both for business and pleasure. Again, the aim is to stay in the best room or suite for the minimum amount of money.

My number one tip is not to phone the Freephone central reservation number unless you really have to. Wherever possible, telephone the hotel directly, as they will always have deals on rates unless they are very busy (which is rare). Most hotels are lucky if their occupancy is 60 or 70% so there are always spare rooms.

Why hotel rooms get discounted

If you are the owner/manager of a hotel and let's say you have 200 spare rooms for tomorrow, if I phone you up for a room for tomorrow and make a sensible offer (I call a sensible offer about 50% to 60% less than their asking price), what would you do? It's better to take a reduced rate than leave the room empty. Don't feel embarrassed to haggle for a good rate and room - I do it all the time and after a while it becomes a habit.

Some hotels now offer free rooms during off-peak times, subject to you paying for breakfast and an evening meal. I think this is very good value because you were going to eat anyway!

Upgrades on rooms

Hotels are very sly and I find that on the whole they never give you a really nice room unless you haggle. When checking into a hotel, never do anything until you see the room first. If you say 'Can I inspect the room first?', in most cases you will get a better room than if you had just checked in.

When you inspect the room, check for things like:

1. Is the room close to a lift/elevator that is likely to be noisy?

2. Is the standard of cleanliness to your satisfaction?

3. Is the bathroom clean and tidy?

4. Is the décor, furniture and room layout to your satisfaction?

5. Is it a non-smoking room? Is there a stale smell of smoke in the air? (One hotel tried to convince me that a room was a non-smoking room when I clearly knew it wasn't, so I asked them to explain

why there were cigarette burns on the furniture and carpet!)

Hotels have different rooms and configurations, so you and I could be staying in the same five star hotel for a business seminar, yet my room could be totally different to yours, so be aware of this. If you are happy after your inspection then that's great, go ahead and sign up. Your rate of tolerance should be offset by the amount of money you are paying and the standard of the hotel; for example, if you're staying in a motorway motel, don't expect a royal suite for £25 a night. At the same time, it should be clean, tidy and fit to stay in.

The problems start when you spend large amounts of money in five star hotels and they try to palm you off with substandard rooms.

If you're not happy with the room

After your inspection, if you're not happy with the room then say so. Express your disappointment and point out the problems; you should then ask to see a better room and/or the HOTEL MANAGER. With a bit of haggling you'll end up with a nice room/suite for an economy price.

Loyalty programmes

Just like airlines, hotels now have loyalty programmes as well, and again, I would join as many as possible. Some hotels do charge a fee, but if you are travelling a lot and you intend to use that chain quite often then it's worth it.

Benefits vary from scheme to scheme, but common benefits are:

1. An upgrade to a junior suite when you book a standard room.
2. Free newspaper.
3. Fruits, gift and drinks on arrival.
4. Complimentary breakfast, evening snacks and drinks.
5. Complimentary use of boardroom and office facilities.

Hotel consolidators

Just like airlines, hotels consolidate as well. As usual, do your own research. Here are a few contact details of hotel consolidators that myself and others have used in the past:

www.travelindustrysecrets.com/Travel_Bonus3.PDF

www.transhotel.com

Interline-UK
4 South Street
Castlethorpe
Milton Keynes
MK19 7EL

Tel: 0845 165 1599 or 01908 510941

HRS - Hotel Reservation Service Ltd.
The Triangle
5-17 Hammersmith Grove,
London W6 0LG
UK
Website: www.hrscorporate.com
Tel: 0208 846 0640
Fax: 0208 846 0641

Buying a few shares in hotels

I own shares in two hotel groups and I receive a special discount card which entitles me to discount room rates, discounts on food in the restaurants (which I can use even when I'm not staying at the hotel) and discounts on health club facilities. As a shareholder you have more power if anything goes wrong, after all, you're a part-owner of the hotel!

Where to find the best hotels in the world

Let's say that it is a special occasion and you want to stay in real luxury, then I would suggest you obtain a copy of *The Leading Hotels of the World* book which is available free from:

UK
The Leading Hotels of the World Ltd
Avenfield House,
118-127 Park Lane
London W1K 7LH
England

Tel: (44-20) 7290-1000
Fax: (44-20) 7493-7773
Email: london@lhw-offices.com
Website: www.lhw.com

USA
Corporate Headquarters
The Leading Hotels of the World Ltd
99 Park Avenue
New York
NY 10016-1601
USA
Tel: (1-212) 515-5600
Fax: (1-212) 515-5899
Email: info@lhw.com
Website: www.lhw.com

This book also contains the telephone/fax numbers, the hotel manager's name, and lots of additional information on all the hotels listed. Hotels that are listed in this book have to work very hard and each member receives frequent rigorous inspections by a team of professional hoteliers. Hotels that are members of The Leading Hotels of the World are very proud to be members and will do anything to keep this title.

If a hotel listed in this book does not meet or exceed your expectations for excellence (which I doubt), then I encourage you to complain. Don't forget, even the world's leading hotels have quiet periods and will discount; many of them have special weekend packages as well.

Summary to getting a good hotel deal

If you take the first thing that is offered to you, which is what most people do, then you deserve what you get; however, if you are willing to politely negotiate and stand up for yourself, then you will be treated with respect and you will end up with a nice room or suite. Don't forget, a hotelier would rather sell a room at a discount than leave the room empty and get nothing, so you've got the upper hand.

How to keep up to date with airlines and hotels

There is a great magazine called *Executive Travel;* it is an American bimonthly magazine published in New York City by American Express Publishing which is available through subscription only, but if you are a regular traveller and own a business, which most of you will be, you should be able to get a free copy by filling in a questionnaire about your travelling habits. For more details write to:

Publicitas
Gordon House
10 Greencoat Place
London SW1P 1PH
Tel: 0207 592 8306
Fax: 0207 5928301

How to hold a meeting and get together at a hotel for FREE

Few people realise that you can use hotel facilities even if you are not staying there. Many business people have conducted many business negotiations in a plush hotel lobby. All you pay for are a few bottles of mineral water or a few cups of coffee. As long as you look smart no one ever troubles you. You can make phone calls in a better environment and send faxes (and receive them), read their newspapers, and make use of their many other services. Always choose a fairly large business hotel; that way you blend in.

Discount car hire

You'll be amazed at the difference in price available from one company to another, or by quoting the right discount code/scheme reference.

On the whole I have always found it cheaper to book car hire before you arrive at your destination; it seems that if you just turn up at the airport unannounced, they just charge you the full going rate. The airline consolidators previously mentioned can give quite good deals on car hire. You can also contact the various firms directly; however, the key is to ask 'Is this the lowest rate available?' and also to look out for promotions that may be offered through your credit card, American Express, or an airline. They normally quote a discount code number which will reduce the quote dramatically, i.e. Hertz has CDP 706770. If you don't have a code, ask the person on the other end nicely and they will normally key one in for you.

In order to save time and money, I usually use price comparison websites on the Internet to look for good deals on anything and everything. The beauty of comparison websites is that you can see all the price quotations under one umbrella before you make an informed decision. For car hire, I have found the following price comparison websites useful:

www.travelsupermarket.com

www.comparecarhire.co.uk

Corporate discounts

Whether you're a one man/woman business or a multinational, you will get a corporate discount if you mention that you own a business and you are a regular user. Car hire firms also have loyalty programmes and if you are a regular hirer, it could be worth getting a card.

NOTE: I personally stick to the larger, well-known car hire firms because I've heard of people's bad experiences with some of the local one-off hire companies; their cars and the service can be very poor and even if they are a bit cheaper, it's not worth it.

Buying electrical goods

I love high-tech electrical goods, such as TVs, computers, games, etc. but I never buy at RRP (Recommended Retail Price) - this is what Jackie Smith pays when she walks into a store, not knowing what she's looking for. The key to discount shopping is to do your research. If, for example, you are buying a video, you should read a few magazines, such as What Video, and become knowledgeable of what's on the market. An informed shopper is a smart shopper; try to know more about the product than the salesman does. Once you know what you want, your task is to find the product at the best price.

Manager's offers/returned goods/ex-display

Nearly all big electrical retailers offer money back guarantees and many people do take the stores up on their offer and return the goods. Now the stores have to resell these goods on and normally offer a 25% to 30% reduction.

My friend recently bought a top of the range DVD player; it was an exchanged product, the instructions had been lost and there was no remote control. Now she knew from her research that the DVD player was very good and retailed for around £450; the store had marked it down to £300 and she made them an offer of £250, which they accepted. The player was fine - it still had a twelve-month guarantee and even carried a seven-day money back guarantee. As for the instructions, she managed to set it up without them and she wrote a nice letter to the manufacturer who sent her a new set free of charge. She got hold of a brand new remote control for £30, so for £280 she had a £450 DVD player - not bad hey! Anyone else can do the same - just keep your eyes peeled for ex-demonstration or returned goods; they offer excellent value and you still have peace of mind with a guarantee.

Shop-soiled goods

I have bought items that were slight seconds and furniture which had a few scratches at greatly reduced prices. The way I see it is, you'll get scratches on your furniture in due course anyway, so what's the difference! Look out for stores that are closing down or having a refit.

How to get money off anything

The easiest way to buy anything at the best price is to research the market. There is always a store somewhere willing to offer you a discount just to get your business; even if it's £10, it's better in your pocket than the store's. The simple thing that people just don't ask is 'Is this your lowest price?' or 'Could you knock something off the price if I buy it today?'

Try it - you'll be amazed by how many small and large stores will take something off for you. Who dares wins!

Buying a nearly-new car at discount

How would you like a nearly new car, normally no older than six to eight months, which still carries all the manufacturer's guarantees and is in excellent condition, for around 30% to 40% off the normal retail price? Well it's possible and the dealers listed on the next page specialise in dealing in these type of vehicles; the only disadvantage is that some of the cars may have a higher than normal mileage.

Where do these cars come from? Many are ex-hire cars because big companies like Hertz and Avis only keep their cars for six to eight months and then they sell them on; some cars are also ex-demonstration, ex-lease cars, or repossessions.

These dealers stock all the major brands, including Ford, Rover, Vauxhall, Nissan, Fiat, and many others.

Cargiant
44-45 Hythe Road (off Scrubs Lane)
White City
London
NW10 6RJ
Tel: 0208 969 5511
Website: www.cargiant.co.uk

Carcraft, Lakeside
Weston Avenue
Tunnel Estate
Lakeside Retail Park
West Thurrock
Essex
RM20 3FJ
Tel: 0800 923 9504
Website: www.carcraft.co.uk

MJA
147 Staines Road West
Sunbury-on-Thames
Middlesex
Tel: 01932 509 979
Website: www.mja-cars.co.uk
Look in Exchange & Mart magazine, available every Thursday for their adverts.

Buying and selling a car

As mentioned above, buying a nearly-new car is a smart way to buy; however, you may wish to buy a car elsewhere and you probably have a car to sell.

Selling your car

If you are looking for the highest price for your car, then in nearly all circumstances, sell it privately through a newspaper or Exchange & Mart. Dealers always offer a trade book price, which is substantially less than the value you could get.

Keys to selling:

1. Make sure the car is clean, both inside and out.
2. Make sure you can prove a full service history and keep receipts of any work you have undertaken, i.e. new tyres.
3. Try to sell the car from spring to September, especially if it's a convertible.
4. If someone makes you an offer below your asking price which you are not willing to take, then keep their number and say you'll get back to them.
5. Answer any questions that the buyer may have truthfully, but don't talk too much, i.e. 'I had an accident a while ago, but it looks as good as new!'

Keys to buying:

These are almost exactly the reverse of selling.

1. Don't get fooled by how clean the car looks; check closely for damage, rust, etc.
2. Ask for the full service history.
3. Try to buy your car around December or January - no one buys cars at these times and dealers are desperate. A great time to buy a convertible is when the weather is really bad.

4. Always get a qualified mechanic, or the AA or RAC to carry out a full inspection before you part with your cash.
5. Get the car checked with HPI (www.hpicheck.com). This tells you if there is any outstanding finance, if the car was a write-off/made up of two cars stuck together, or is stolen.
6. Buy with your head and not only your heart; if you smell a rat or something just doesn't sound right then walk away - your instincts are normally right.
7. Think about the insurance group - the engine size and model, such as GTI, can make a big difference to the premium.

There's a saying in the motor trade: What do you think about XXX car? The answer depends if you're buying or selling!

If the motor trader is buying the car in they'll say, 'Oh, this is a bad model; high insurance and prone to rust'. Now if they are selling the same car to you they would say, 'Great, popular model, economical, sporty engine!'

Try to research the market before you buy or sell a car. Get hold of a few of the latest car magazines and read up; an informed and knowledgeable consumer is a smart buyer.

Buying, selling and exchanging

There are now a few legitimate companies who buy, sell, and exchange all sorts of electrical goods, household goods, computers, jewellery, records, tapes, CDs, videos, etc.

When I recently moved house I had quite a few items that I didn't really want and instead of throwing them out, I took them to one of these stores and got cash for them. As well as making you money, it is also environmentally friendly; I think we throw away far too much.

Before I go any further, these stores are legitimate - they will only buy goods from you that are yours, i.e. NO STOLEN GOODS. You will be required to provide ID and the stores have video surveillance.

These are the two main ones I know of; however, I'm sure there are others.

CASH CONVERTERS
Cash Converters (UK) Limited
Innovation House
Aston Lane South
Preston Brook
Cheshire
WA7 3FY
Tel: 01928 737410
Website: www.cashconverters.co.uk

CASH GENERATOR LTD
CG House
Express Trading Estate
Stonehill Road
Bolton
Lancashire
BL4 9TP
Telephone: 01204 574444
Fax: 01204 577711
Website: www.cashgenerator.co.uk

CeX
The Old Brewery
Hille Business Centre
132a St Albans Road
Watford
Hertfordshire
WD24 4AE
Website: www.uk.webuy.com

As well as selling your unwanted goods, you can also see what other goods they have which may be of interest to you.

Chapter 16

Choosing where to live, buying/selling a property and mortgages

For most people their biggest living expense is their rent or mortgage. The cost of housing varies dramatically from one part of the country to the other; for example, an average one-bedroom flat in London buys you a nice five-bedroom house with some land in many other parts of the country.

For many people, work dictates where they live, yet with the types of businesses that I have outlined in the money making section, this is no longer a problem - you can work on a remote farm, as long as you have a phone/fax and a postbox fairly nearby.

Do think about moving out of highly-priced cities; I have lived in cities and in countryside locations and on the whole, I find that the countryside does offer a better standard of living. If you miss the city you can always go on day trips or stay a few nights in a hotel.

As well as lower rent and property prices, you'll also find that insurance premiums, both for your car and home, are slashed when you move out of big cities and big towns.

The decision about where you want to live is yours, but do think about it because this could be a big money saver. For many, they prefer a main residence in the countryside and a small flat in the city - this way you get the best of both worlds.

Renting

First of all, renting a property is a mug's game! You are basically paying someone else's mortgage for them; some people rent for years and at the end of it they have nothing to show for their money. Renting is a good temporary solution, but is foolish in the long term. It is better for you to be the landlord or landlady, and to take in a lodger or two and get them to pay your mortgage for you. A good friend of mine does this; he has three lodgers and he also lives there as well. The lodgers pay enough rent to cover his mortgage, electricity, gas and his food bill, so he's basically living there RENT FREE with no living expenses. Now the great benefit of this is that he's building up an asset. His property has increased in value and his mortgage is going down, so one day he will own the property outright and it will have been paid for by the lodgers.

Buying a property at the right price

For many, buying a house/flat will be the biggest investment and decision that they will ever make, yet I have seen individuals buy a house or flat with little care, concern or research. They see a property, their heart rules their head and before you know it, they have bought themselves a pile of trouble. As if this isn't bad enough, they then go and get bad mortgage advice and end up with a terrible mortgage to add to their problems.

Now you may have had some problems with property ownership in the past or you know someone who has, but by using some common sense pointers, you can avoid costly mistakes.

Let me tell you what type of properties sell well and those that don't. You see, when you buy a property you should be thinking about the resale potential. The chances are that you won't want to live there forever, and although I cannot guarantee that you'll make a profit from your property, I would hope that you can at least get back the money you paid for it - today you are the buyer, but one day you will be the seller.

Properties that SELL WELL

1. Houses with four bedrooms
2. Houses with a reasonable amount of garden, but not too much land as this can put many people off

3. Houses with a bedroom that has an en-suite bathroom
4. Houses in a cul-de-sac
5. Houses that have good open countryside views
6. New houses or houses that are a few years old
7. Detached homes
8. Houses in a good condition that are close to amenities
9. Houses with good central heating, preferably gas

Properties that are HARD TO SELL

1. Older houses (some older 1970s styles are very out of fashion)
2. Purchased council estate houses
3. Three bedroom houses
4. Small houses in remote villages (larger houses sell better)
5. Houses on a main road
6. Small flats
7. Flats over shops
8. Large houses on small plots (houses that are overlooked are bad news)
9. Houses that don't have good central heating
10. Houses with old electrics and plumbing

11. Flats with high management/maintenance fees

Now let's say that you've found a property you like, let me tell you what I would want to know:

1. Are you buying the property with your head and not your heart?
2. Why are the current owners truthfully selling? How long have they been there? And how much did they pay? (You can find out if they won't tell you, through Land Registry.)
3. Are there many houses for sale in that area?
4. Is there anything you should know about, i.e. a new airport, motorway, or fire station across the road?
5. Take a walk around the area at different times and also walk past or drive past the house at different times - is there anything strange happening? Pop into a local shop and while buying something, casually mention that you are thinking of moving into the area and buying a house in XXX road; you'll be amazed at what you can find out, i.e. 'He's just lost his job' or 'Their business is going through a rough time'.
6. Are the current owners desperate to sell? How long has the property been on the market? Find out how many different agents are trying to sell the property. (If a house is being offered

by many different estate agents, then I guarantee you that they are desperate to sell.)

7. Think hard about why you want the house and how long you plan to be there for.

8. Try and find a comparative property to get a guide price; this means a similar property in a nearby area that has sold in the last six to twelve months.

9. If you are buying a flat, check the management fees and ask for the last three years of accounts of the management company; find out what the annual rate of increase in management fees has been. Also, are there any possible large expenditures coming up, such as a new roof or redecoration of the hallway? If you buy a flat, you are liable for a percentage of these costs.

Making an offer

Let's say that you're now happy with the property and subject to the survey/searches, you need to make an offer which is a good deal to you, yet not so ridiculously low that the vendor will think you are a total joker. My view is that there should be at least 10% off the asking price. Whatever offer you make, don't ever make your final offer straight away, for example, if the most you can afford is £125,000, don't make this offer first; offer £120,000 and hopefully you'll settle at £122,000.

NOTE: Try not to show your true feelings, either with the estate agent or the vendors. Say you are interested, but never show that you are desperate to buy the property. If an agent says that they have had other offers, then call their bluff and walk away, and ask the agent to show you another property.

Summary to buying a property

I could probably write a whole book on this subject, however, I hope you will find my pointers useful. You have to live somewhere and as long as you buy with your head, you should be able to make a profit on the property or at least break even. Remember to go against the flow; people tend to move house in the spring or summer, but if you are willing to buy and move in during the winter months, you'll normally be able to get an extra few thousand pounds off the price.

When everyone is talking about property (e.g. the property boom of 1988 and 1989 in the UK) then that's the time you should be a SELLER. You should be a buyer when everyone else is SELLING, for instance, between 1991 to 1993 there were excellent bargains in the property market in the UK because so many property companies were going broke and people were panic selling.

Paying your mortgage off quicker/getting a better deal

Most people take out a mortgage over 25 years; however, if you have to take out a mortgage, I suggest you take one out for 15 to 20 years maximum. You see, although your payments will be slightly higher, you will be paying back less accrued interest. If you have a current mortgage you could contact your lender and ask them to adjust the term.

The key to a mortgage is getting it paid off as quickly as possible. If you have some spare cash you can always pay off a bit extra on your mortgage; some people pay a few extra payments a year to reduce their balance quicker. Contact your lender for further details on how to make extra payments towards your mortgage.

Getting a better deal

If it was a long time ago that you took your mortgage out, you could find that another bank or building society could provide you with a better deal, and even though there may be some fee and hassle in changing over to a new mortgage lender, for many it's worth it. You could also find that just by phoning your existing lender up and telling them that you've seen a lower rate elsewhere, they will renegotiate your mortgage interest rate. You see, if you have been a good customer they will not want to lose you.

A guide to getting a good mortgage or remortgage

Firstly, remember that you are buying a product. Borrowing money is just like buying anything else: take the first offer that is given to you and you'll be paying too much; however, with some research and a bit of haggling you can cut your monthly mortgage payments quite dramatically.

Here are my points to follow:

1. Check the small print. Can you pay off or change the mortgage without a penalty? If there is a penalty, how much is it? Are there any other conditions, such as compulsory insurance requirements etc.?

2. The best deals are available to those who have at least a 25% deposit to put down or those who are switching mortgages and are only asking for 75% or less of their current property's value.

3. If you are a first-time buyer, then make sure that you get an extra discount.

4. In most cases you can buy buildings and contents insurance cheaper through another source than your building society. However, sometimes it is best to play dumb and take theirs if you will benefit from a much better mortgage deal. Also, some lenders say that you only have to take the first year's buildings and

contents insurance through them, thereafter you can go elsewhere.

5. Do make it a priority to ensure that your mortgage is paid on time because a bad mortgage reference will mess up your chances of getting a good deal in the future. If you hit problems, then tell the building society/bank immediately and make whatever payments you can.
6. Don't deal through a mortgage broker unless you really have to.
7. If you need to know where you stand, then a fixed rate mortgage could be for you, either for part or the entire term of the mortgage. For example: A fixed rate mortgage of 7% for ten years means, regardless of whatever happens to interest rates, you only pay the rate.

Repayment methods

There are two main ways you can pay off your mortgage. They are as follows:

Repayment mortgage

This is the straightforward method where you pay the interest and capital off on a monthly basis for an agreed period. At the end of the term that's it, you've paid everything off.

Interest-only mortgage

With an interest-only mortgage you make monthly repayments for an agreed period but this will only cover the interest on your loan. This means in five, ten, or twenty years' time you will still owe the lender the same amount you initially took out. You will normally also have to pay into another savings or investment plan that will hopefully pay off the loan at the end of the term.

Summary

Because a mortgage will probably be the largest amount of money you will ever borrow in your life, take your time and do your research. There are many good magazines on the market, such as What Mortgage, Which Mortgage, and Moneywise.

Chapter 17

Shares, investing, pensions and savings

The easiest way for you to become wealthy is to start putting money away on a regular basis; whatever your position, even if it's £50 a month, get into the habit of saving and investing. As you start making more money I would suggest that you put away at least 30% of your annual income. If you can discipline yourself to put away more, then that's even better. You may say that it's hard to save money and yes, I agree, especially when you're earning a small income; however, it must be done. You need to face up to the fact that one day you won't be able to work, even if you want to. Don't expect the government to look after you because the way things are going, I doubt if there will be a state pension by the time many of us retire.

You need to look after yourself and you need to start saving today. If you have a good income coming in when you're older, your standard of living will be much better - you will be able to afford private medical care, you can have a nurse, a maid, a chauffeur, etc. The last thing you want to have is money worries when you're older.

Why you should be a saver and an investor

The old saying is: money makes money. If you start building up some extra capital, with time, and by making smart investments, you could be increasing that capital by around 15% to 20% per annum. These figures are realistic and some investment companies return a lot more than this.

Let me show you how £1,000 can grow over ten years:

Year 1	£1,200
Year 2	£1,440
Year 3	£1,728
Year 4	£2,073
Year 5	£2,487
Year 6	£2,984
Year 7	£3,580
Year 8	£4,296
Year 9	£5,155
Year 10	£6,186

So put in simple terms, £1,000 turns into over £6,000 in ten years, which isn't as long as you think. Now here's the best point about investing: on the whole you don't need to do much, you just wait. Some people may be thinking that a bar of chocolate will cost more in ten years' time, so £6,000 won't be worth much, and it's true that you do have to think about inflation; however, I assure you that unless you are living in Russia or some other unstable economy, inflation does not run at 20%.

Once you build up enough capital, you will never have to work again if you don't want to - you can simply live off the interest and investment income. As I've already mentioned, in your old age you may not be able to work even if you want to.

How to invest your hard-earned money

First of all I want to tell you that investing money is FUN. Can you honestly tell me that you don't find turning £1,000 into £2,000 interesting and fun?

The keys to good investing:

1. Take a medium- to long-term view. Quick results are nice, but the real way to make big returns is by being patient, consistent and by keeping your head. Work on a five to ten year time frame.

2. Spread your money around and never put all your eggs in one basket. I'll talk about asset allocations later, but you basically need a mixture of investments and you always need some liquid cash which can be withdrawn on

instant access or seven days' notice for emergencies.

3. Be sharp and don't fall for any scams like 500% returns from ostrich farming or a guaranteed 10,000% increase in penny shares within six months! Yes, there are some wonder stocks and I'll talk more about them later, but they are the exception and not the norm.
4. Think hard about whom you invest your money with. Do lots of research, read books, attend courses, and learn as much as you can about smart investing.

A pension plan

For most people a private pension plan should be their first investment. A pension plan has tax advantages that are worth taking. Carry out your own research into top-performing pension companies; Sunday newspapers, such as the Sunday Times and the Telegraph, carry a lot of information on pension companies; also read the Investors Chronicle. Your monthly contribution, i.e. £50 or £200, will depend on how much you want to achieve at the end of the pension.

NOTE: Take the time to choose the right company to use for your pension plan; don't just walk into your high street bank and buy theirs because there is a chance you'll get short-changed. Many of the top performers are specialist pension fund managers that are not necessarily household names.

Unit Trusts, Mutual Funds, Pooled Investments and Individual Savings Accounts (ISAs)

I have always liked these types of investments because there is a fairly low entry level and you get a balanced investment in lots of different shares, instead of buying one share directly.

Let me explain how a Unit Trust/Mutual Fund works. A bank/fund manager sets up a fund (let's call it the ABC American Growth Fund); when they set up the fund they lay out objectives, such as to invest in American companies who offer medium growth. They then market the fund to individuals like yourself and with the money that you and other individuals send them, they then invest this on your behalf to obtain maximum returns. Now they make their money by charging a management fee.

Now let's say that you invest £2,000 in this fund. You will be buying units in the fund and let's say each unit costs £1, so you now have 2,000 units which you can buy or sell. The units will go up or down depending on how the fund is doing. Let's say that your fund owns XYZ shares and they get taken over at a much higher price than the fund manager bought them for - the fund has therefore made a profit and in turn your units will increase.

At the same time, if your fund manager makes bad investments then your units will go down.

How to choose a good unit trust

Again research the market - most Sunday newspapers carry league tables of the best and worst performing trusts. Now I must warn you that PAST PERFORMANCE IS NO GUARANTEE FOR FUTURE PERFORMANCE, but if a fund has been doing well consistently for over five or ten years, then the chances are it will continue to do so.

A good source of information in the UK is the Investors Chronicle which I've been buying for years. It comes out every Friday and is available from most big newsagents (it can also be found in big libraries). You'll see many adverts for unit trusts in the Sunday papers; send off for information and make your decisions based on your own research.

Don't forget that you can invest in as many different funds as you wish, so you could invest in a steady growth fund with one company and then invest in a more speculative technology fund with another company.

The pros and cons of a unit trust

Pros

1. It gives you the chance to invest in markets which are difficult for you to trade in as a private investor, for instance, Latin America, Poland, Taiwan, etc.
2. It works for the 'don't put all your eggs in one basket' principle. Your fund will be divided into lots of stocks; therefore one bad investment will not sink the whole fund.
3. You don't need to monitor your investments on a daily basis as your fund manager does this for you. The fund manager also has the expertise and better access to information and resources than a private investor has.

Cons

1. You don't have a say in how your money is invested.
2. You can feel out of control.
3. There are some terrible fund managers out there and some funds who underperform dramatically in the market. I recently met someone who invested £5,000 over five years with a large household name and ended up, after costs, with about £4,900. He would have been better off leaving his hard-earned money in a building society.

On the whole the pros outweigh the cons, and you can keep an eye on your unit prices by either phoning the company up for a quote, or by checking the Financial Times. Most fund managers will also send you a regular update on how the funds are doing. If your fund manager is constantly underperforming in the market and is at the bottom of the league tables, then take your money elsewhere - every fund has its ups and downs but there is a limit.

Individual Saving Accounts (ISAs) - UK only

This is a tax-free investment account which replaces the Personal Equity Plan (PEP). You can invest a maximum of £5,000 per tax year in any tax year. In the 2012/2013 tax year you can invest £5,600. On the whole an ISA works like a unit trust and there are some self-select ISAs that allow you to choose some of the shares in your ISA.

Should I take financial advice?

You may have noticed that so far I haven't told you to take any financial advice - on the whole I think you should steer clear of financial advisors and learn to deal with your own affairs. Only seek financial advice if you are desperate and even then, take it as an opinion and not a fact. This statement will upset a lot of people who make their money from charging fees and commissions, however, I think it is only fair that I reveal to you why your best interests are not always in the mind of most financial advisors.

Firstly, most financial advisors aren't independent. They're not really even allowed to call themselves that because they are employed by big financial fund managers or insurance companies and they are only allowed to sell their company's products, so they are SALESMEN. Many are ex-car salesmen, estate agents, double glazing salesmen, etc. so do you really want to invest your hard-earned cash based on their advice?

What about those wonderful independent financial advisors (IFA)? Well they are a bit better, but they're still salesmen and they need to earn commissions to live. You see, many of the best funds to invest in are the ones that DON'T PAY any commission to salesmen/IFAs and the chances are that you won't be recommended any of these!

Note: There are a few financial advisors who you pay by the hour for advice. They will not sell you anything and they will not take any commission - if there is any commission earned they will give it back to you. This is quite a fair way to do business.

The best financial advisor you'll ever meet is YOU; after all, no one cares more about your money than you do.

Risk + Reward

The easiest way to put this is: if you leave all your money in a bank or building society your risk will be minimal, however, so will your reward.

Now unless you are a thrill seeker, I don't suggest you plough your life savings into a new technology penny share; however, at the same time you shouldn't leave your money just sitting in a building society.

Savings accounts and banks/building societies

As previously mentioned, you always need to have some cash that you have access to either very quickly or immediately. The key to getting the highest return is to shop around because the rates of interest on savings can vary dramatically from one institution to another. The smaller building societies tend to offer better interest rates; however, you may not have a local branch so it would mean dealing by post.

Investing in shares

Dealing in shares has become cheaper and easier in the last few years. Today almost anyone can open an online account with a stockbroker like Charles Schwab and trade immediately.

What you need to know about shares

Firstly, shares go up as well as down and because of new technology, shares are traded more aggressively than they were in the old days of the Stock Exchange floor; this means that even a relatively safe share can move sharply higher or lower in a matter of 30 minutes.

Now although there have been some stock market crashes (mainly 1929, 1987, and 2000), on the whole, shares over a long period are investments. I also want to point out that whether we are in a BULL MARKET, which means that shares on the whole are in an upward trend, or in a BEAR MARKET, which means that shares on the whole are in a downward trend, there are always opportunities and you can still lose lots of money in a bull market and make lots of money in a bear market.

FTSE 100 INDEX

This index consists of 100 most highly capitalised blue chip companies listed on the London Stock Exchange. The companies in this index includes Aviva, Barclays Bank, BP, Aggreko, Burberry, Next, Sainsbury, etc.

FTSE 250

The index comprises of mid-capitalised companies not included in the FTSE 100. The companies in this category include Betfair Group, Dairy Crest, Debenhams, Greggs, Halfords Group, Ladbrokes PLC, etc.

What shares should you buy?

Well firstly, we've mentioned that many hotels and airlines give discounts to shareholders, so depending on your circumstances you may want to buy shares in a company that you use regularly, especially if they offer a discount.

On the whole, most investors will be looking for shares of medium sized companies, normally listed in the bottom half of the FTSE 100 or the FTSE 250. These are companies that provide growth, but do not have the risk factor associated with the smaller stocks.

Research and furthering your knowledge

The Investors Chronicle is a good source of information on companies and they also give regular share tips; however, be warned that Investors Chronicle also gets it wrong at times! Investors Chronicle is respected and is heavily read in the city. An excellent TV station that I strongly advise you to watch regularly is CNBC; this station is available on satellite and cable TV throughout the UK and Europe. I watch this channel regularly and you can learn so much from watching. Most stockbrokers and fund managers have TVs in their offices with CNBC on or watch CNBC on their computers. Up till 2 p.m. this channel covers the UK and the European markets; from 2 p.m. till 11 p.m. it covers the US market; then throughout the night it covers the Asian markets and at weekends they have excellent business and computer programmes.

I would also suggest that you learn more about why companies go up and down, what dividends and price/earnings ratios are, etc. There are many good books and courses on this subject and I suggest you take a trip to the library or a good business bookshop. There are also various seminars on investing and tax planning.

If you would like to know more about investment courses then you can complete the feedback form at the back of this book and I will point you in the right direction.

Space does not permit me to write everything there is to know on shares, however, I hope you will look into this further. Shares can make you extremely wealthy; for instance, if you had bought only 20 or 30 shares in Apple or Microsoft about 10 or 15 years ago, you would now be wealthy!

The random method of picking shares

This may sound totally mad but it's a fact that if you were to open up the Financial Times at the share price listings in the back, close your eyes, and point to ten different shares at random, the chances are that you will outperform many city brokers and fund managers over five years!

Making money from penny shares

It is everyone's dream to pick a share that's worth a few pence and for it to skyrocket into pounds and before you know it, your investment of a few hundred pounds has turned into thousands. Well it does happen and I've picked my fair share of them; however, I must warn you that you can also lose your complete investment; therefore, if you do want to try your hand at penny shares, then only invest what you can afford to lose.

What you need to know

Firstly, a penny share is normally a company whose shares trade at anything from 1p to 60p. Now let's get this clear, it doesn't mean that the company is cheap because it is trading at a few pence. Without getting too technical, a company can change its share price by issuing more shares (a script issue), which gives the impression of a share price going down, or they may opt for a consolidation, which gives the impression of the share price going up.

The key to valuing a company is its market capitalisation (as I already mentioned in FTSE) - this is the amount of shares in issue multiplied by the current market price. You see, a script issue puts more shares into the market and a consolidation takes shares out of the market and although the share price will change, the capitalisation will not - it's just how you divide the cake.

Why shares trade in pennies

The two main reasons are that either it's a small company and new to the market, therefore it's trading at a low share price, or it was a pound share at some stage and the company has hit bad times and the share price has crashed.

How to make money with penny shares

The two basic scenarios of making money are:

A) It's a small company, possibly a new company, which has little track record but does have prospects, for example, a new product, a new wonder drug or a new piece of computer software. I know people who have invested in small oil exploration companies in the past, which have done very well when they struck oil. The other way you make money with a penny share is a takeover bid; this is when a bigger company wants to buy out the company you have shares in and they offer you a higher share price to sell.

B) This scenario takes the view that a big company, who was successful, hits rough times and the share price crashes. Now this doesn't always happen, but it's possible that with some time and new management etc., the company can start to rebuild; even if the company does not go back to where they were before, you can still make large profits.

Let me give you a true example: A British retailer called Next plc, did very well through the 80s but hit bad times in the early 90s. The shares had been trading at £3.00 a share and because of problems and losses, they became a penny share. A friend bought Next plc at 11p. His view was this:

1) The worst that could happen would be if they were to go broke and he would lose all of his money, which was a relatively small investment at 11p a share.
2) Someone would take them over and pay more than 11p a share for them.
3) They would recover.

Anyway, as some of you will know, Next didn't go broke - in fact the last time I saw the share price it was over £31.00 a share! That's not a bad return;

it took around 15 years for the price to go from 11p to £31.00.

Another advantage of a penny share is that you can buy more of them for your money. For example, 10,000 Next shares cost my friend £1,100 when he bought them and today they would cost him over £310,000.

How to buy and sell shares

The easiest and cheapest way is to open an account with a stockbroker like Charles Schwab Europe if you are in the UK or Charles Schwab in the US. For details on opening an account with Charles Schwab Europe, phone 0800 917 1039. Schwab can buy and sell all UK traded companies and they are also able to trade US companies. They are an execution-only broker, which means that you call the shots. A full list of stockbrokers can found in the Investors Chronicle.

Tax planning and claiming benefits

Most people don't claim what they are entitled to; they either don't know what they are entitled to or can't be bothered. The chances are that there is a grant or benefit that either you or your business could be entitled to. If you have been unemployed and you are now starting your own business, then you will definitely be entitled to a grant. If you're going back to work after having a baby, you should also be entitled to some benefits, including free training in computers.

Again, space does not permit me to go into depth on this subject; however, you can start to research what you may be entitled to. Watch out for companies who promise to get you a grant or benefit for your business in return for a large upfront fee - in many cases they'll take your money and run, or provide you with worthless information.

The other point with grants and benefits is that they are always changing, but with your own research you should be able to track down what you are entitled to.

Tax planning

One of the biggest savings that you can make is by finding ways to pay less tax. There are many legal tax loopholes that are used by wealthy individuals to reduce or even eliminate their tax liabilities. As an employed person you have less possibilities open to you than if you are self-employed or a company director; however, you can still ensure that your employer is deducting tax and national insurance at the correct rate. Ensure that your tax code is correct because you may find that you have been overpaying for years.

As for the self-employed and company owners, I suggest that you get hold of a book called *The*

Green Book which was written by lawyers, chartered accountants and former tax inspectors. The book will give you a true understanding of offshore companies, trusts, avoiding Capital Gains Tax, protecting your assets and much more. Even if you are not super rich, as long as you are making a fairly good income you should be able to offset setting-up fees and management fees against tax savings. More details about the book are available from: SCF Group, Scorpio House 102 Sydney Street, London SW3 6NJ.

Cheaper motor insurance and home insurance

Motor insurance

The main areas that can make a difference to your motor insurance is where you live, your occupation, your driving records and of course, the value of your car. Here are a few tips to follow:

1. Make sure that you are using the right postcode - it can make a big difference to your premium.

2. If you are willing to meet the first £250 of a claim (excess) instead of the normal £50, you will find that you can reduce your premium.

3. If you are a low mileage motorist, then you should be able to get a lower premium. Ask insurance companies for low mileage discount schemes.

4. Deal directly with the insurance company and not through a broker, as this cuts out commission.
5. Do phone around as the difference can be incredible and don't just accept your current insurer's renewal quote, check the premium every year. Just because XYZ was dearer last year, it doesn't mean they won't be cheaper this year.
6. Make sure the insurance company has you grouped in the right occupation band.
7. Never lie on an insurance form or over the phone - if you need to claim and the insurance company finds out, they are legally entitled not to pay out.
8. Make sure the insurance is legitimate; they say that you only know how good the company is when you come to claim. Also make sure that your insurance company offers a FREE courtesy car; if your car is in a garage for two weeks you'll need a car and hiring is expensive.

Household insurance

Many of the tips are as above, except:

1. Some insurance companies now offer 'no claims' bonuses on household insurance as well and if you have a good record this can make a difference.

2. Make sure that you are fully insured but are not paying for insurance that you don't need. Some companies offer block insurance of say £25,000 for contents and if you only have £10,000 worth of contents, then you could be paying for too much cover.
3. Shop around and beware of taking buildings and contents insurance from your bank or mortgage lender as they tend to be expensive.
4. Some insurers offer an 'excess' on home contents, so if you are willing to pay the first £100 of the claim you can reduce the annual premium.
5. Just like motor insurance, make a note to review your household insurance as things change; don't accept your current insurer's renewal quote without comparing it to others at the time.

Compare insurance prices

Comparing insurance prices does not need to be time consuming. There are a few free websites where you can get the best deal by comparing multiple insurance quotes from various insurance companies at the same time; this is all under one website for your convenience. This helps you immensely by saving you valuable time and money. Some of them include the following:

www.gocompare.com

GoCompare compares over 125 insurance companies and over 80 leading home insurance companies.

www.moneysupermarket.com

MoneySupermarket compares cheap car insurance quotes from over 100 companies and cheap home insurance from over 80 companies.

www.comparethemarket.com

Comparethemarket.com compares hundreds of prices from top car insurance providers and home insurance from over 50 home insurance providers.

www.confused.com

Confused.com compares over 120 leading motor insurers and over 80 leading home insurers.

www.uswitch.com

They compare quotes from over 120 car insurers.

Chapter 18

Buying designer clothes for less

For most of us, we cannot justify spending hundreds, if not thousands, on one suit or dress; however, there is a way to get designer fashions with up to 60% off RRP (Recommended Retail Price) every day of the year and that's by shopping at designer outlets and shopping villages. You will be amazed to see all the famous names, including Ralph Lauren, Mulberry, Prada, Austin Reed, Burberry, Charles Tyrwhitt, Hugo Boss, DKNY, Nike, Timberland, Thomas Pink, Paul Smith, Tommy Hilfiger, Vivienne Westwood, etc.

Shopping Villages/Outlet Centres

There is a new trend in consumer shopping habits. Instead of buying from retailers in high streets, town centres, etc. consumers can go to a shopping village or an outlet centre, where manufacturers sell their products directly to the public through their own stores. This way, consumers can now afford to buy their favourite designer clothes directly from the manufacturers at heavily discounted prices. This is a new trend in consumer shopping habits and a smart way to save money. There are shopping villages all over the United Kingdom and in Europe, namely: Austria, Belgium, Czech Republic, Denmark, France, Germany, Holland, Hungary, Portugal, Republic of Ireland, and Sweden.

For more details on your nearest shopping village, visit their website:

www.shopping-villages.co.uk

Aldo Outlet
231-233 Camden High Street
London NW1 7BU

Burberry Outlet
29-31 Chatham Place
Hackney, London E9 6LP
Tel: 020 8328 4287

Sterling Mills Outlet Shopping Village
Tillicoultry
Clackmannanshire
Scotland
FK13 6HN
Tel: 01259 752100
Website: www.sterlingmills.com

Tweedmill Shopping Outlet
Llannerch Park
St Asaph
Denbighshire
LL17 0UY
Tel: 01745 730 072
Website: www.tweedmill.co.uk

Junction One International Outlet Shopping
111 Ballymena Road
Antrim
BT41 4LL
Northern Ireland
T: 028 9442 9111
Website: www.junctionone.co.uk

Clarks Village
Farm Road
Street
Somerset
BA16 0BB
Telephone: 01458 840 064
Website: www.clarksvillage.co.uk

Cheshire Oaks Designer Outlet
Kinsey Road
Ellesmere Port
South Wirral
CH65 9JJ
England
0151 3485600
Website: www.cheshireoaksdesigneroutlet.com

Bicester Village
50 Pingle Drive
Bicester
Oxfordshire
OX26 6WD
Tel: 01869 323200
Website: www.bicestervillage.com

Springfields Outlet Shopping
Camelgate
Spalding
Lincolnshire
PE12 6EU
Tel: 01775 760 909
Website: www.springfieldsshopping.co.uk

Ashford Designer Outlet
Kimberley Way
Ashford
Kent
TN24 0SD
United Kingdom
Tel: +44 (0)1233 895900
Website: www.ashforddesigneroutlet.com

In addition to the shopping villages and designer outlets there are permanent discount stores that sell brand labels at discounted prices.

London area:

Browns Labels for Less
24-27 South Molton Street
London W1K 5RD

Tel: 0207 514 0016
Website: www.brownsfashion.com
Stock mainly comprises of leftovers from previous seasons, including Issey Miyake, Genny, DKNY, MaxMara and Moschino.

The Salvage Shop
96-100 Watling Avenue
Burnt Oak
HA8 0LR
Middlesex
Tel: 0208 952 4353
Stock is mainly from loss adjusters from premises that have been flooded or suffered fire damage. Lots of well-known brands.

Choice Discount Fashion Store and Home Store
West London Branch:
Unit 11 Arcadia Centre
Ealing
London W5 2ND
Tel: 0208 567 2747
Website: www.choice-discount.co.uk

TK Maxx
Aberdeen Branch
Aberdeen Union Square
Union Square
AB11 5PF
Tel: 01224 583000
Website: www.tkmaxx.com

Hawes & Curtis Outlet
594 Green Lanes
Turnpike Lane
London N8 0RA

Bradleys
85 Knightsbridge
London SW1 7RB
Tel: 0207 235 2905
There is a permanent half-price application on La Perla lingerie, swimwear and nightwear. Stock is mostly end-of-line.

Discount Dressing
39 Paddington Street
London W1U 4HH
Offers literally hundreds of new designer fashions, normally obtained from bankrupt businesses, cancelled orders, or over-makes.

Change of a Dress
294 Broxtowe Lane
Nottingham NG8 5NB
Tel: 01159291531
Very upmarket stock, including many of the big fashion names.

Seconds Out & New Too
High Street, Cookham
Berkshire SL6 9SQ
Phone & Fax: 01628 850371
Website: www.secondsout.biz

Offers middle to upper class range of designer labels, including Karl Lagerfield, Versace, and Chanel.

Designer sales

These are not permanent outlets and you should contact them to find out the date of the next sale and the location.

Frock Me
Tel: 020 7254 4054
Website: www.frockmevintagefashion.com
The fair offers a good selection of designer names for both men and women. The fair also offers accessories.

The London Designer Sale
Contact Tracy on 07900 432661
Website: www.thelondondesignersale.co.uk
The sale takes place four to five times a year in Central London. Attendance is usually by invitation so make a point of asking to be placed on the mailing list.

Dress agencies

Up till now we have concentrated on new and nearly new clothing; however, there are a number of excellent dress agencies that buy, sell and exchange designer clothing. Most of the clothing has hardly been worn and offers excellent value for money. If you have quality designer items that you no longer wear, trade them in - you can receive cash or exchange them for something else, or you can of course just buy if you have nothing to sell.

Pandora Dress Agency
16-22 Cheval Place
Knightsbridge
London SW7 1ES
Tel: 0207 589 5289
Website: www.pandoradressagency.com
Pandora is the leading exponent in the resale of the most pristine, gently used, designer clothing and accessories. Well worth a visit and it's only a few minutes' walk from Harrods.

The Frock Exchange
7 High Street
Fenstanton
Cambridgeshire
PE28 9LQ
Tel: 01480 461187
Website: www.thefrockexchange.co.uk
For a full listing of dress agencies check in the back of Vogue magazine.

Men's agencies and discount outlets

Although the market is mainly geared towards ladies, there are a few men's discount outlets.

Chapter 19

Buying from auctions and wholesale

Most people have never been to a legitimate auction and are really missing out. Before I go any further, I stress legitimate auctions because there are some companies who call themselves auctioneers, but are really just sales companies.

Contrary to popular belief, anyone can go to most auctions and they don't just sell deceased estates, house clearances, and general junk (although there are some auctions like this). There are also auctions who offer the following:

Lost/stolen unclaimed property and seized goods

These are the government auctions, with many items coming from the police, HM Revenue & Customs, British Rail, etc. These auctions tend to offer a wide range of goods.

Bankruptcy and liquidation stock

These auctions consist of brand new stock: raw materials like clothes or screws, and office/manufacturing equipment. I was at a recent auction for a sportswear company that had gone broke; all the clothing was brand new and still had price tags on it. The clothes were being sold for around 30% of the retail value.

Job lots and end-of-line products

This is where big name manufacturers clear out their warehouses of seconds, end-of-line products and mail order returns.

What you need to know about auctions

The best type of auction is one that has no reserves. This is common with government auctions and it means that if there is an item no one else is interested in, you can bid £1 and walk away with it. You see, big auction companies don't have the time or space to hold stock, they just want to get rid of it.

Finding good auctions

First of all, some of the better auctions tend to be held on weekdays and not weekends, as this stops the casual bargain hunter going. Look in your Yellow Pages for a full listing of auctioneers or search the Internet and try to get on their mailing list. I have listed a few auctioneers here:

Southgate Auction Rooms
55 High Street, Southgate, London N14 6LD
Tel: 020 8886 7888
Website: www.southgateauctionrooms.com

Centaur Auctions
Centaur House, Harbet Road, Lea Valley Estate, Anthony Way, Edmonton, London N18 3HR
Tel: 020 8803 9796 Fax: 020 8807 7111
Email: centaur9@btconnect.com
Website: www.centaurauctions.co.uk

The Swindon Auction Company
98 St. Austell Way, Swindon, Wiltshire SN2 2DG
Tel: 01793 873307 Mobile: 07505 362953
Website: www.swindonauctionco.co.uk

Kerr and McAlister

48 Cogan Street, Auldhouse Retail Park, Off Nether Auldhouse Road, Glasgow, Lanarkshire G43 1AP

Tel: 0141 649 5710

You will find the following websites useful for a full listing of auctioneers in your area. If you are serious about auctions then I suggest you subscribe to a newsletter, such as the Government

Auction News.

www.wholesalescout.co.uk/police-auctions

www.ukauctionguides.co.uk

www.police-auctions.org.uk

Government Auction News
Wentworth Publishing Ltd
17 Fleet Street
London EC4Y 1AA
Tel: 020 7353 7300
Fax: 020 7353 6533
Website: www.wentworth-publishing.co.uk

How an auction works

Once you know the time and date of the auction you will be able to attend the viewing session; this could be the day before the auction or a few hours before. This gives you the chance to have a good look at the items, which are known as LOTS. Each lot will be marked with a number - make sure that you write this down as most auctioneers lump items together, for example, 20 assorted videotapes = Lot 10.

After the viewing you will normally need to get a Bidding Card. This is obtained by putting money in an account, normally £50 or £100. If you don't buy anything then you get your money back at the end of the auction and if you spend more than your deposit, you pay the difference.

Bidding at auctions

First of all, do make sure you are bidding for the right item - listen to the lot number and the description. The auctioneer will then open with something like 'Do I have a bid of £50?' and if there is no answer, he will come down until a price is accepted by someone; then the price starts moving upwards again.

TIP: Set a maximum price in your mind that you're willing to pay for the lot and do not go over that. I've seen many people at auctions getting carried away and they end up paying far too much.

Unlike what you see on TV, you don't scratch your nose or raise your eyebrows to bid; the main way is to raise your hand with your ticket number; the auctioneer is well trained to spot bids, even in a crowded room, and will look your way. If yours is the winning bid the auctioneer will say, 'Sold to the gentleman/lady on the right' and he will normally ask you for your bidding card number - that's how they know it's you.

Gaining experience at auctions

My advice is to go to a few auctions and watch other people. Most people at auctions are quite friendly and will often help you out with any questions you have.

NOTE: Most auction houses want their money straight away, preferably in cash. In some cases they will hold the goods for one day so you can come back, but usually no longer than this. They also expect you to take the goods away within a day, as they need the space. Some auctions can arrange for delivery of big items but there is a charge for this.

Summary

Auctions can be a very good way to buy new and used goods at low prices. Keep your head when bidding as it's easy to get carried away. Auctions can be very lucrative if you are interested in buying and selling; many items bought at auctions can be sold on at a profit through local adverts or to your friends and family.

Office products, stationery, envelopes etc.

If you are running your own business, which most of you will be, then I strongly recommend that you get an account either with Office Depot or Viking Direct if you're in the UK (including Ireland and the Channel Islands). They deliver to your door, normally the next day, and their prices are very competitive. Both Viking Direct and Office Depot sell nearly everything you can possibly think of that your business will need, including photocopier paper, envelopes, pens, packing materials, office furniture, fax machines, photocopiers, toner cartridges for your laser printer, and even coffee.

Viking Direct Ltd
Bursom Industrial Park
Tollwell Road
Leicester, LE4 IBR.
Tel: 0844 412 3435
Website: www.viking-direct.co.uk

Office Depot UK
501 Beaumont Leys Lane
Leicester LE4 2BN
Tel: 0116 237 2001
Website: www.officedepot.co.uk

Buying at wholesalers

One of the big advantages of owning your business is that you can get membership to wholesalers and buy goods at greatly reduced prices. Now contrary to what most people think, you don't have to buy a minimum of 2,000 tins of baked beans or a ton of sugar at a time; most wholesalers sell in packs of 6 or 12; as for electrical goods and many other items, you only have to buy one.

There are many wholesalers all over the country - check your local Yellow Pages or search the Internet. The two wholesalers that I have listed sell almost everything at substantially reduced prices. Items include food and drink, electrical goods, household goods, toys, DIY items, gardening goods, CDs, computers, and many other items.

Makro

Access to these warehouses is by membership only; there is no fee for Makro. To join you'll need some proof that you are in business, i.e. a business bank statement, telephone bill, or letterhead.

For more details contact customer services on 0161 7884 700 or 0844 445 7445. For information on your local Makro branch, visit their website www.makro.co.uk

Costco

Costco Wholesale is an American membership warehouse club with 22 stores in the UK. It is dedicated to bringing its members quality goods and services at the lowest possible prices. They sell food, electrical goods, clothes, and many household goods at extremely competitive prices. To find the nearest branch call the Costco head office on 01923 213 113 or visit their website: www.costco.co.uk

Please find the following useful websites:

www.wholesalers365.co.uk

www.simplywholesale.co.uk

www.booker.co.uk

www.thewholesaler.co.uk

Chapter 20

Banking and credit cards

In the making money section I warned you about banks overcharging on business accounts and cheques being cashed twice and bank charges etc. I want to remind you again to watch out with your personal bank accounts.

The main item to watch out for on personal accounts is direct debits. Is the same direct debit being taken out of your account twice and is it the correct amount? Also, if you cancel something, make sure that the direct debit/standing order is cancelled on the correct date as many companies will sneak an extra month through!

No fee credit cards

In this day and age we all need a credit card - have you ever tried to book a flight, hire a car or buy something on the Internet without one? It's almost impossible.

There are so many offers on the market these days; most providers offer a no fee credit card that will not charge you an annual fee. It also used to be possible to get a balance transfer no fee credit card, but lenders have now started implementing a small transfer fee for the privilege of the interest-free period. However, you should check the terms of the agreement to ensure you won't be charged more for something else in replacement of the fee.

Things to consider when looking for a no fee credit card include:

- Are they recouping the fee elsewhere? E.g. in the interest rate.
- Will you be charged more for defaulting on payment or going over your limit?
- Is there an interest-free balance transfer period and what is the fee? (They're usually about 2-2.5%)
- Will you receive a 0% interest period on purchases or is that forsaken for the no annual fee?
- Never agree to a credit card without first shopping around and reading the conditions of the agreement.

To find the no fee credit card that will best suit your needs, there are a few free comparison websites where you can compare the best deals on credits cards from different financial institutions. They are as follows:

www.moneysavingexpert.com
www.money.co.uk
www.compareandsave.com
www.moneysupermarket.com

Cut the cost of your telephone calls

Telephone call charges have dropped dramatically both in the UK and in the USA; however, you can still save money by using prepaid calling cards and independent telecom companies.

Most telecom companies offer competitive packages on telephone lines, so as usual, shop around before you make an informed decision. There are a few comparison websites where you can compare different local and international calling rates from various providers on their websites. Some even offer a better deal when you get your broadband from them. They include the following:

www.moneysupermarket.com
www.simplifydigital.co.uk
www.homephonechoices.co.uk
www.comparethemarket.com/compare-home-phone/
www.uswitch.com/broadband/compare/broadband_and_home_phone/
www.cheapestinternationalcalls.com
http://www.niftylist.co.uk

Calling cards

Calling cards offer great discounts to many countries, including North America, South America, Europe, Africa, Asia, virtually everywhere across the globe. Another good reason to have a calling card is that it's much cheaper to phone home when you're away; you don't have to worry about hotel telephone surcharges or lots of coins to put in a phone box.

Summary on saving money

I would like to sum up this section by saying that learning to spend and invest wisely is the key to holding on to your wealth and it's the key to making your money last. Many people think that rich people don't haggle or ask for discounts, yet the truth is that it's partly because of their careful spending that they ever accumulate any wealth in the first place.

Rich people are not misers - they enjoy spending their hard-earned money on themselves and loved ones but they ensure that they get the best deal they can; this way, they can have their cake and eat it! They get tremendous satisfaction when they get a discount, upgrade, or a special bargain.

Do learn to take charge of your financial life and learn to invest your money wisely. Money does make money and as I have previously outlined, a relatively small sum can grow into a considerable amount over time.

Use the information in this book to your advantage and you too can make your hard-earned money go further. It has definitely taken me years to learn these secrets from wealthy people around me; I have been applying them ever since and this is the first time that I have ever shared them.

I am always happy to learn about new money saving schemes and discount outlets, so if you either own a business or you have a favourite discount outlet, then drop me a line and I will add it to the next reprint.

Chapter 21

Joy of salvation

As a Christian author, the purpose of this book will not be fully accomplished if it does not give people the golden opportunity to give their lives to Jesus Christ and to acquaint themselves with Him. A fool says that there is no God, and that Heaven and Hell do not exist. But what if you are wrong? What if God and Jesus really exist? Don't you think it would be wise to live your life as if God, Jesus, the Holy Spirit, and Heaven exist than to live your life in denial and end up in eternal damnation? Brethren, if you believe and submit your life to Jesus Christ today, you lose nothing - in fact you gain everything (eternal home in Heaven). Jesus does not force us to believe in Him, though He could. Moses told the Israelites "I have set before you life and death, blessing and cursing: therefore choose life, that both thou and thy seed may live." Deuteronomy 30:19 (KJV).

Jesus has provided sufficient proof of His existence for us to willingly respond to Him. The creation of the universe, the earth's perfect distance from the sun, the unique chemical properties of water, the human brain, DNA, the number of people who attest to knowing God, the gnawing in our hearts and minds to determine if God is there, the willingness for God to be known through Jesus Christ, and the inspiration He gave to men to write the Bible. The evidence that God the Father, God the Son (Jesus) and God the Holy Spirit exist is ginormous. This is a contemplative issue and not to be taken lightly; as a matter of fact, it is a case of life and death.

The value of your soul

Jesus asked His disciples over 2,000 years ago, "For what is a man profited, if he shall gain the whole world, and lose his own soul? Or what shall a man give in exchange for his soul?" Matthew 16:26 (KJV).

Beloved, Jesus is asking me and you this question today - what have you got or are about to acquire that is worth trading for your soul? Just what is the value of your soul? Jesus says here that your soul, my soul, one person's soul, is worth more than the whole world. Can you imagine this? Your soul is worth more to God than the entire world. Let me tell you something:

According to the Credit Suisse Global Wealth Report published in 2012, the total combined wealth of the entire planet was $223 trillion, and it was projected that this will increase to $345 trillion by 2016. These are all tangible assets in the world.

The United States of America alone, where the New York Stock Exchange is based, is described by Wikipedia as the world's largest stock exchange by market capitalisation of its listed companies at US$14.242 trillion, as of December 2011. In addition, the Bank for International Settlements confirmed that US$4 trillion is traded daily in global foreign exchange markets.

In comparison, Carlos Slim Helu, presently the richest man on earth (according to www.forbes.com), is not able to exchange his soul with his US$69 billion wealth. Do you have this kind of wealth? None of us do. Besides, even if you had the wealth of this entire world, according to Jesus, it still would not be enough.

Let me give you a few reasons as to why all this world's wealth cannot buy your soul into heaven.

- First, the wealth of this world is temporary. We are told that all things here on this earth are temporary and will pass away. How many of you would accept as payment for a debt, money that had value for only a short amount of time. None of you. Why should God, with all of his wealth, accept something that is temporary in value?

- Secondly, God owns it all anyway. How can you exchange something for your soul that does not truly belong to you anyway? You just have temporary use of what you have. Everything on this earth was created by Him and for Him, for His glory. In other words, it is already His.
- Thirdly, and the most important reason, is that the exchange has already been made. Jesus Christ exchanged himself on the cross for your soul. He died a vicarious death so that you and I would not have to endure the wrath of God. You see, God knew we could never exchange anything for our souls. So He did it for us. He gave his own son.

"For God so loved the world that He gave His only begotten Son, that whosoever believeth in Him should not perish but have everlasting life." John 3:16 (KJV)

Can you put a price on the Son of God? God did. I believe that God had such love for man that if Adam were to have been the only man ever created, God would have given His son to save His soul. You see, that price was in reality just one soul.

The exchange for our souls was made some 2,000 years ago. Jesus knew what He was asking; He knew that man could give nothing of any value, that man alone possessed nothing for exchange. There is one thing however, that we all have, that we can give in exchange for our souls. That thing in its own right has no value whatsoever. No value until the exchange is made, and then it is of infinite value. That thing that we can give in exchange for our souls is our acceptance and belief in the lord Jesus Christ.

Jesus asked the question: what shall a man give in exchange for his soul? He knew that He Himself would be the answer. He knew that it was He who would lay down His life in exchange for our souls. He knew that God the Father would accept nothing else. Jesus gave His all. That is what it takes.

We cannot save ourselves. Our own righteousness is like filthy rags in the sight of Almighty God. In conclusion, I hope you realise that the only thing that you can give is to accept Jesus as your personal Lord and Saviour. There is absolutely nothing else on earth that will be of enough value to exchange for your soul. I beseech you brethren to give your life to Jesus Christ today. Be at peace with your Maker today. The occurrences happening all over the world indicate the second coming of the Lord is imminent.

Don't delay

Today is the day of salvation because tomorrow might be too late. Salvation is found in no other name. Before you can truly occupy till He comes, you need to know Him and have a personal relationship with Master Jesus. Do you want to know Him? If the answer is YES then I congratulate you because you are still alive and have the chance to know Him. He is waiting earnestly and tenderly for you to come to Him today. He said that He will in no wise cast out all who come to Him. It does not matter what your race, gender, or status in society is, nor how great your sins are. In fact it is because of our sins that He died for us. The Bible says when we were sinners Jesus died for us, and for this purpose, the son of God was made manifest to destroy the works of the devil.

Confession

All that is left for you is to accept the gift that Jesus is holding out for you right now. The Bible says "If you declare with your mouth, 'Jesus is Lord', and believe in your heart that God raised him from the dead, you will be saved. For it is with your heart that you believe and are justified, and it is with your mouth that you profess your faith and are saved." Romans 10:9-10 (NIV).

To give your life to Christ, say the following prayer and accept Jesus as your Saviour.

Prayer

Say this loud and clear:

Dear Lord Jesus, I come to you today a wretched sinner; I believe that you died on the Cross of Calvary and rose from the grave on the third day to give me eternal life. I believe that you are the only way to Heaven. I am very sorry for my sins and I sincerely repent of my sins. Please forgive me, have mercy on me and wash away my sins in your precious blood, in Jesus' name. (Amen)

Welcome

Congratulations! Welcome into God's family. Heaven celebrates and rejoices with you! The Bible describes how there is joy in the presence of God's angels when you commit your life to God. I am ecstatic that you have taken the bold step to follow Jesus. My friend, you have done the right thing. This is not the end, this is just the beginning. You need to nurture your relationship with the Lord Jesus by reading your Bible every day. Please find a Bible-believing firebrand church so you can worship God with other brethren. God bless you and uphold you to the very end in Jesus' name (Amen). I would like to present you with a free e-book to help you in your new journey. To receive this free e-book please send an email to me at occupytilljesuscomes@gmail.com and your free e-book shall be emailed to you.

Have you backslided?

"The backslider in heart shall be filled with his own ways." Proverbs 14:14 (KJV)

Have you backslided? Have the distractions and cares of this world taken your focus away from looking unto the author and finisher of your faith? Backsliding is not necessarily getting drunk or committing adultery, or any outward course of sin seen by the public. Backsliding is in the heart! Dear Beloved, it may be that you have drifted somewhat but have never noticed it. You may be like Samson who "wist not that the Lord was departed from him" (Judges 16:20). We need to search our hearts and we need to watch and pray lest sin creep up on us.

"Thine own wickedness shall correct thee, and thy backsliding shall reprove thee: know therefore and see that it an evil thing and bitter, that thou hast forsaken the Lord thy God, and that my fear is not in thee, saith the Lord God of hosts."

Jeremiah 2:19 (KJV)

In the story of the prodigal son that Jesus illustrated in the book of Luke 15:11-32, the prodigal son came to his senses and said in verse 18 "I will arise and go to my father. And will say unto him Father I have sinned against heaven and before thee." And in verse 20 the boy "arose and came to his father". We are told that "when he was yet a great way off, his father saw him, and had compassion, and ran, and fell on his neck and kissed him."

What an amazing lesson for anybody who wants to come to God! Whether a lost sinner who wants salvation or a backslider who wants a renewed right spirit and a restored joy of salvation, the Bible says that "if we confess our sins, He is faithful and just to forgive us our sins, and to cleanse us from all unrighteousness." John 1:9 (KJV)

One observation that I have made is that among some brethren during the time of confession of sins, you will hear them speaking in tongues. Beloved, I want to ask you a question: when you were committing that lustful sin in your heart, were you speaking in tongues? If the answer is no, why should you now start blowing tongues? To do so is an absolute deception. If you are easily provoked and get angry quickly, confess the sin of anger; if yours is holding grudge, say it as it is. Beloved, let's call a spade a spade and not an agricultural implement.

We need to ensure that we do not excuse our sins, nor make an alibi for them, nor cover them up. "He that covereth his sins shall not prosper: but whosoever confesseth and forsaketh them shall have mercy." Proverbs 28:13 (KJV). May we receive mercy from God in Jesus' name (Amen). Any honest confession will mean that we must have a penitent heart that turns away from sin with shame.

Beloved if you feel like weeping, you may weep. One could imagine how the prodigal son must have wept bitterly when he came home. I speak from experience when I was a 'Hotch Scotch Christian' - that is, I was neither a hot nor cold Christian. Praise God of many chances that had mercy and findeth out me. Whether there is weeping or no weeping, let us remember that "The sacrifices of God are a broken spirit: a broken and a contrite heart, O God, thou wilt not despise." Psalm 51:17 (KJV)

When you have sincerely confessed your backsliding, then you ought to believe that God has forgiven you as He has promised.

Jesus, our first Love

"Unto the angel of the church of Ephesus write; These things saith he that holdeth the seven stars in his right hand, who walketh in the midst of the seven golden candlesticks. I know thy works, and thy labour, and thy patience, and how thou canst not bear them which are evil: and thou hast tried them which say they are apostles, and are not, and hast found them liars: And hast borne, and hast patience, and for my name's sake hast laboured, and hast not fainted. Nevertheless I have somewhat against thee, because thou hast left thy first love. Remember therefore from whence thou art fallen, and repent, and do the first works; or else I will come unto thee quickly, and will remove thy candlestick out of his place, except thou repent." Revelation 2:1-5 (KJV).

Beloved, if the church at Ephesus could lose its first love, so can we! Perhaps many of us have; we need to stop and remember that joy of salvation, that moment when we gave our lives to the Lord Jesus. We need to repent of the things that have come between us and the Lord. This world is passing away with all its lusts and desires.

The whole duty of Man on earth

Ecclesiastes is one of my favourite books in the Bible, written by King Solomon. He was described as a person great in wisdom, wealth, and power. In his quest for the meaning of life he wrote this extraordinary book. He wanted to find out why he was alive, why he was created. He tried knowledge, wealth, experience and everything and he called them all vanity upon vanity.

After all the wrangling of the dialogue of the book of Ecclesiastes, King Solomon said everything has been said that has to be said on the subject.

"Let us hear the conclusion of the whole matter: Fear God, and keep his commandments: for this is the whole duty of man. For God shall bring every work into judgement, with every secret thing, whether it be good, or whether it be evil."

Ecclesiastes 12: 13-14 (KJV).

When one considers everything that King Solomon has written, one would get down to the essence of living. That's actually what "the whole duty of man" means - it's the essence of life. It's taking away everything that's extraneous and boiling it down to core things, as follows:

- Fear God. It's something that he said all throughout the book. To fear God isn't to cower. Fearing God means that we know who He is and where we stand in relation to Him. It means taking him seriously, acknowledging Him in our lives as the highest good. It means revering Him, honouring Him, and worshipping Him.
- Keep His commandments. This is what life is about. The most important thing for anyone to do is to worship God and obey his commandments. We were made to worship and obey. God told the Israelites to leave Egypt so that they might worship Him.

It is sad to see how some people live their lives as if Jesus is not coming back again; some people even say that when we die that's the end. Apostle Paul told the Corinthians that if in this life only we have hope in Christ, we are of all men most miserable. It reminded me of a story that was told many years ago about some children in a family that gathered around at Christmas time in great anticipation of opening their Christmas presents. The presents had been voluptuously wrapped with ribbons, and the kids were excited. Paper began to fly everywhere as they hurriedly unwrapped all of their presents. The presents had cost a lot and they had been well packaged. With great vim and vitality, the children began the process of unwrapping them. However, when all the gifts had been unwrapped, one of the children asked, "Is this all there is?" Evidently, some of us have experienced that. Many of us have unwrapped life and we want to know if this is all there is. Yes, there is more life in Jesus, as in the book of John 10:10 (KJV), Jesus told his disciples, "I am come that they might have life, and that they might have it more abundantly." He came that we might have abundant life now and later on for all eternity.

Beloved, let us cast away all those small sins that easily beset us. Let us live on earth as the children of the kingdom. Let us remember that one day God shall sit in judgement and the books shall be opened; every case will have to stand the test of the law. God has a law by which He governs intelligence, both in Heaven and on earth. Jehovah is the supreme Judge of nations. "For God shall bring every work into judgement, with every secret thing, whether it be good, or whether it be evil." Ecclesiastes 12:14 (KJV)

In closing beloved, occupy till He comes in the things of the Lord; be your brothers' keeper. Love God with all your heart till it hurts, love the unlovable, share your wealth with the disadvantaged, visit the widows and the fatherless. "Pure religion and undefiled before God and the Father is this, to visit the fatherless and widows in their affliction, and to keep himself unspotted from the world." James 1:27 (KJV)

Let us be up and doing and be passionate about the work of the Lord because the second coming of the Lord is at hand. Occupying till He comes should cause us to evangelise and make disciples of the nations as Jesus commissioned us to. "And He said unto them, go ye into all the world, and preach the gospel to every creature." Mark 16:15 (KJV)

Don't say the Lord is coming and I'm just going to sit here and wait for Him to take me home - NO please don't do that - that's selfish and displeasing unto God. We that are saved should rise up for the salvation of others. Work hard like never before for the Lord while it is yet day because the night cometh, when no man can work.

May God richly bless you as you continue to follow Him and occupy till He comes. May we all reign with Him eternally in Jesus' name. (Amen)

"Now unto him that is able to keep you from falling, and to present you faultless before the presence of his glory with exceeding joy, to the only wise God our Saviour, be glory and majesty, dominion and power, both now and ever. Amen."

Jude 1:24-25 (KJV)

Chapter 22

The final summary

Beloved, we have finally come to the end of this book. The Bible says that better is the end of a thing than the beginning thereof. I am delighted that you have bought and read this book. I'm sure you will agree with me that this book is the foundation for a successful life. I have thoroughly enjoyed writing this book. Take the time to study and put the principles discussed into action every day for the rest of your life and you will build strong and broad foundations which will allow you to build the highest skyscraper of success, wealth, and happiness. Skimp on the foundation and whatever you try to build will always be shaky and in the majority of cases, it will topple over. Too many people rush into business or try to make money without understanding the basic principles of putting your life in order first; without sound health, both physical and mental, and a balanced lifestyle, money will not come your way and even if it does, it will not fulfil you.

I have disclosed some life-changing tools in this book and if used correctly, you too can start to achieve your dreams. However, remember this is a journey and you will need commitment, perseverance, and vision to overcome obstacles, including the many sceptics and doubtful people that you will meet along the way.

It is easier to give up than carry on, especially when things don't appear to be going your way, but by giving up and admitting defeat, you join the ranks of the other millions of life's losers and no-hopers who are living shallow, empty and worthless lives, hoping that Lady Luck will help them win the lottery!

Now although success does take some effort, it really is worth it and I speak from first-hand experience. Remember that you have a long way to go yet and reading this book is only a tiny step up a long ladder that you need to climb; however, now that you've started, keep going.

God richly bless you as you occupy till He comes in the name of Jesus. (Amen)

"Now unto him that is able to do exceeding abundantly above all that we ask or think, according to the power that worketh in us." Ephesians 3:20 (KJV)

Where do we go from here?

Well we have come a long way and if you've worked your way to the end of this book, then pat yourself on the back and congratulate yourself. If you genuinely use the information that I have revealed to you in this book then you will be on the road to an incredible journey, but please remember that achieving the success you deserve is a journey and you have a long way to go yet. The next and final section is the reference section where I have listed various addresses, telephone numbers and books which will be of value to you.

Is it over?

I hope not! Firstly, I would love to hear from you and you will find a questionnaire at the end so you can air your views about this book. Please TAKE THE TIME TO COMPLETE THIS FORM. I'd love to hear your success stories and with your permission I could even incorporate them into the next reprint of the book and if I do, I'll send you a personal copy.

The next step

I have put everything that I could print into this book; however, there are many things that I cannot describe in printed words - I need to show you visually, you need to hear my voice and see my facial expressions. I cannot guarantee when or where, but I will be holding about two to three seminars a year, and as a reader of this book, I would invite you to attend. The seminar will be full of action-packed information where I will go through many of the points outlined in this book, together with many new concepts and ideas. I will also be happy to answer your questions and give advice. I intend to keep the seminar numbers fairly small and I want them to be as private as possible. If you are interested in attending then please drop me a line and I will put you on the mailing list; I will then send you further details as and when they are available. I know that there will be more people who will want to attend that I can take; however, I will work on a first come, first served basis.

Register today FREE of charge and receive regular updates and a free e-book

By simply completing and returning the form at the back of this book by email, I will keep you up to date with all the latest news and any changes. I will also send you a free e-book called *How to Acquire a Millionaire Mindset* which you will find invaluable.

Reference Section

Olukoya, D.K. (2010) - *The Prayer and Deliverance Bible* published by MFM Publications

Olukoya, D.K. (1999) - *Prayer Rain* published by MFM Publications

Hendrickson (2008) - *The New Hendrickson Parallel Bible* published by Hendrickson Publishers

Dake, F.J. (1999) - *The Dake Annotated Reference Bible* published by Dake Publishing

Strong, J (2010) - *The New Strong's Expanded Exhaustive Concordance of the Bible* published by James Strong Publishers

Macarthur, J (2007) - *Macarthur Study Bible*

Yonggi Cho D. (1996) - *Holy Spirit My Senior Partner* published by Charisma House - ISBN-13: 978-0884192268

Renner, R (2003) - *Sparkling Gems from the Greek* published by Harrison House Publishers - ISBN-13: 978-0972545426

Munroe, M - *The 7 Principles of the Eagles* - Internet Article

Karbo, J (1986) - *The Lazy Man's Way to Riches* published by Success Classics Library – ISBN 1-884337-22-8

Trump, D (1997) - *Trump: The Art of the Comeback* published by Times Books - ISBN 0-8129-2964-0

Stanley, T.J. & Danko, W.D. (2010) - *The Millionaire Next Door* published by Taylor Trade Publishing

Hill, W.G. (1994) *Think Like A Tycoon* published by Scope International - ISBN-10: 0906619300

McCormack, M.H. (1989) - *Success Secrets* published by HarperCollins –ISBN 0 00215186 3

Popeil, R - *The Salesman Of The Century* – ISBN 0-385-31378-0 published by Delacorte Press

Caples, J (1998) - *Tested Advertising Methods* published by Prentice Hall - ISBN-13: 978-0130957016

Ogilvy, D (1985) - *Ogilvy On Advertising* published by Vintage ISBN-13: 978-0394729039

Bland, M (1987) - *Be Your Own PR Man: Practical Public Relations for the Small Business* published by Kogan Page - ISBN-10: 1850914176

McDowell, C (2002) - *Ralph Lauren: The Man, The Vision, The Style.* Rizzoli, New York

www.concordances.org

www.wikipedia.org

www.helpsbible.com

www.dictionary.com

Introductory Pack on Funding and Finance – Procurement and Contracting – A guide to the rules and procedures that constitute public sector procurement

Pre-Qualification Questionnaire for tender evaluation – useful guidance from the Office of Government Commerce

Good Magazines

Investor Chronicle (UK)

Entrepreneur International

Business Week

Income Opportunities (USA)

Marketing Week

Exchange & Mart (UK)

The Trader (UK)

Internet Access

Most telecom companies offer good deals on broadband packages. Here are a few comparison websites where you can compare tariffs before you choose a provider:

www.uswitch.com

www.moneysupermarket.com

www.gocompare.com

Interesting websites

www.bloomberg.co.uk or www.bloomberg.com

This is a great place to check all your UK AND US share prices.

www.google.co.uk or www.google.com

This is an excellent search engine. You will often hear people say 'I'll Google that question' e.g. 'What's the meaning of life?' and many answers will then pop up. You can keep up with the rest of the world and read local and international news. You can also create an email account e.g. abc@gmail.com

www.yahoo.com or www.yahoo.co.uk

Another good search engine; it can be used to search information and to get quotes on share prices. Read national and international news. You can also create an email account e.g. abc@yahoo.co.uk or abc@yahoo.com

www.entrepreneurmag.com

This is the electronic version of my favourite business opportunities magazine. Although it is mainly aimed at the US market, you will still find lots of useful business information that can be used regardless of where you live.

www.hilitedms.co.uk

My list brokers site. Good place to research mailing lists.

www.godaddy.com

A good site to register your domain names or to check if a domain is available.

www.amazon.com

The world's biggest online bookshop, carrying over five million books, including many old and hard to find books.

Office stationery and business supplies

Viking Direct Limited
Bursom Industrial Park
Towell Road
Leicester
LE4 1BR
Tel: 0800 424 444 Customer Services: 0800 424 445
Fax: 0800 622 211

Mailing list broker

Hilite Limited
Ash House, Ash Road
New Ash Green
Longfield
Kent DA3 8SA
Tel: 01474 874 848
Fax: 01474 879 292
Other list brokers are listed in BRAD Direct Marketing.

Feedback about this book

Help me to help you and receive a FREE e-book and regular updates

However good myself and others think this book is, I am always ready to improve and listen to reader's suggestions. I also love to read letters from readers who have changed their lives by putting the information in this book into practice, so if you have anything to say then please drop me a line.

Please take a few minutes to complete and return this form. Once completed you should email it to occupytilljesuscomes@gmail.com

Once received, we will send you a free e-book as a thank you and we will send you regular updates, as and when.

Name:
Address:
Postcode:
Tel:
Email:

What did you think about this book? Making money, business secrets, increasing your pay, saving money and the joy of salvation?

Excellent ☐ Good ☐ Average ☐ Poor ☐

(Please tick one)

A) Helped me to start my own business

YES ☐ NO ☐

B) Helped me to increase my pay

YES ☐ NO ☐

C) Helped me to decide that I was working in the wrong job

YES ☐ NO ☐

D) Helped me to increase my current business profit

YES ☐ NO ☐

E) Helped me to know Jesus

YES ☐ NO ☐

Please feel free to write any other comments in this section:

____

____

____

____

____

____

____

Have you used any or all of the methods to buy goods or services at discounted rates?

YES ☐ NO ☐

If yes, did you use the information to save on (please tick all relevant boxes):

Airlines ☐
Hotels ☐
Car Hire ☐
Clothing ☐
General Goods ☐
Car Purchase ☐
House Purchase ☐
Insurance ☐
Telephone Calls ☐
Broadband ☐
Stationery ☐
Others ☐ (Please specify)

Please write a few words on what you think about this book as a whole:

____

____

____

____

____

____

____

Would you be interested in future details on (please tick all relevant):

Seminars ☐ Other books ☐ Consultation ☐

E-books on Internet marketing ☐

THANK YOU! I APPRECIATE THE TIME THAT YOU HAVE SPENT COMPLETING THIS QUESTIONNAIRE AND IT WILL BE READ BY ME PERSONALLY. YOUR FREE E-BOOK WILL BE EMAILED TO YOU.

God richly bless you as you seek to occupy till He comes in Jesus' name (Amen).

"WHEN THE LORD TURNED AGAIN THE CAPTIVITY OF ZION, WE WERE LIKE THEM THAT DREAM. THEN WAS OUR MOUTH FILLED WITH LAUGHTER, AND OUR TONGUE WITH SINGING: THEN SAID THEY AMONG THE HEATHEN, THE LORD HATH DONE GREAT THINGS FOR THEM. THE LORD HAS DONE GREAT THINGS FOR US; WHEREOF WE ARE GLAD."

PSALM 126:1-3 (KJV)